Turn Aga

D0618513

After the death of someone near to us, we come to a fork in the road. At that crossroad, we must make a significant choice. We can go either to the left or to the right. Often neither of these is what we really desire.

If we had our preference, we would have the parent, friend, mate, or child back with us again. However, that is impossible. Death is final, and the road for the departed one has ended.

Another choice has to be made. How will the future be lived without one's loved one? In most cases the choice is either to turn away from life or to turn again to life.

If a loved one was turned away from life by death, then why should the survivor not turn away from life also? This road is marked by pain, depression, despair, and even wanting to die. To take this road briefly is a natural response to a loss. But turning away from life cannot be a permanent choice. At some point one must take the other fork marked hope, optimism, and renewal.

The central message of this book is that people can choose the unnatural direction after any death—no matter how tragic—and turn again to life.

If I should die and leave you here a while,
    Be not like others, sore undone,
Who keep long vigil by the silent tomb and weep.
    For my sake, turn again to life, and live . . .
Nerving your heart and hand to do
    that which will comfort other souls than thine.
Complete these dear, unfinished tasks of mine.

—Author Unknown

TURN AGAIN TO LIFE

Growing Through Grief

Abraham Schmitt

HERALD PRESS
Scottdale, Pennsylvania
Kitchener, Ontario
1987

Library of Congress Cataloging-in-Publication Data

Schmitt, Abraham.
  Turn again to life.

  Bibliography: p.
   1. Bereavement—Religious aspects—Christianity.
2. Death—Religious aspects—Christianity.   3. Consola-
tion. I. Title.
BV4905.2.S3   1987   248.8'6   86-33581
ISBN 0-8361-3436-2 (pbk.)

TURN AGAIN TO LIFE
Copyright © 1987 by Herald Press, Scottdale, Pa. 15683
   Published simultaneously in Canada by Herald Press,
   Kitchener, Ont. N2G 4M5. All rights reserved.
Library of Congress Catalog Number: 86-33581
International Standard Book Number: 0-8361-3436-2
Printed in the United States of America
Design by David Hiebert; cover from Anchor/Wallace

92 91 89 88 87 10 9 8 7 6 5 4 3 2 1

DEDICATION

As a practicing individual and family therapist, I have shared in the struggles of many persons as they experienced grief—the final painful separation from one whom they have loved.

I have watched and I like to think that I have helped—as they have tried to avoid and then outrun the enemy we call grief. I have been there, too, as many of them have turned courageously to face the enemy.

I have been privy to their grappling, observing helplessly at times while grief seized them and threatened to strangle what was left of their lives.

My heart has sunk when some of them have gone under.

I have cheered when others have bravely returned to the sunlight and life.

This book is a testimonial to their courage—a therapist's fond salute to all who have dared to face this enemy and have won the victory!

CONTENTS

AUTHOR'S PREFACE

Death has not pursued me, so I have pursued it. At this time in my life my parents are alive and relatively healthy. My seven siblings are fine. In my immediate family I have experienced no loss. Then why am I so fascinated with death?

From infancy to adulthood I lived in a peasant village in Saskatchewan, Canada, where death and grief were exposed for all to see and to experience. There were no hospitals, no homes for the aged, no funeral homes. Aging, dying, and preparation for burial occurred at home. These life events were everyone's concern—dramas played out for all to see. As children we could not be sheltered from the most painful events. If we cared to watch the women prepare the body for burial, that was our privilege. If we were present we also heard the sad laments or the final relief in the ending of this earthly life. I was especially interested in how the village carpenter built the coffin, since I was a carpenter's apprentice and assumed I would be the builder of coffins later.

Even as we watched the grave being dug in the village cemetery, we heard the men telling and retelling the life story of the deceased. This was their attempt to deal with the loss. The daily reporting of any dying or grieving process was heard by every child. All the stages from birth to death were lived naturally and let go of naturally.

After I left this society and assumed my role as an individual, in marriage, and as family therapist and teacher, I sensed a huge missing piece in sophisticated American society. There was no natural death talk here. No matter how developed the culture, everyone was as finite as the people in the village. They simply did not deal with it. Infirmity, death, and grief still occur, only they happen in sterile institutions handled only by appropriate professionals. The more these are not openly experienced, the less people talk about them, and more harm is done to the persons who must still experience them. With this awareness I became a teacher on death, dying, and grief.

My goal was to take the peasant message and translate it into modern language. The first step was to teach an interdisciplinary course on death and dying to a broad selection of helping professions at the graduate level of a university. This caused students to discover the close correlation of life and death. To make peace with death is essential to live fully. Therapists need to know about the ending of life before they can help people to claim life. At this point I wrote the book *Dialogue with Death* (out of print).

Following the release of that book more people saw me as a death therapist. My client load shifted to include more persons suffering from acute loss and grief. The time seemed right to write another book on this subject. I wanted to show how to grow through grief.

It is my hope that by using many case illustrations I will accomplish three things. I want people to begin to contemplate losses before they occur, so that when they experience them they will have more resources to cope with the loss. I desire that those who are struggling with a loss may find direction for coping in a more productive way. My final hope is for readers to gain courage and insight to reach out to those around them who are coping with grief. The central message is that grieving persons need us more than ever before. They already feel abandoned. They do not need us to increase their loneliness.

There is a developmental order to the chapters of this book. The first two chapters deal with the excruciating loss through teenage suicide. Pastor Craig Landis, the father, tells his side of the story. Then in Chapter 2 Anne intimately shares her side of that story.

In Chapter 3 I describe the phases of the grief process. Then in Chapter 4 Martha Troyer shows us how she turned to life after she assumed she was dying but instead her husband died.

In the following chapter I show why we need to choose repeatedly to collide with death in order to live. The theme of Chapter 5 was the central message of my earlier book.

I was most fortunate to have the privilege of walking with Joyce Fischer as she guided her two young sons through the sudden accidental death of her husband and their father. She shows us how to deal sensitively with children as they act out their own unique style of grieving in Chapter 6.

Unfortunately, not all people die well nor do they then help the survivors grieve well. Such a sad situation is described in Chapter 7. This is the only illustration where the names and material have been disguised to protect the survivors who have not yet fully turned again toward life.

Mary Ann in a most courageous way shows us how her battered heart found the strength to go on after dealing with too many deaths. Chapter 8 forces one to grapple with grief.

Throughout the decades of dealing with grief I have developed a model for walking with people through this phase of life. It has proved effective for other therapists as they adopted this model for treating those needing help through grief. This grief model is described in Chapter 9.

In Chapter 10 some material is repeated from my earlier book. A highly unusual event which came to my attention following the use of this earlier chapter is included.

Many people have learned to know and love Sara since she came out of hiding to tell her story of a loss which occurred many years ago. As she told it we all became participants in the helping process and rejoiced to see her turn from captivity to freedom. Her story is shared in Chapter 11.

In the final chapter I summarize the message of the book which is also the message of The Book of Life. In turning again to life we can really trust that neither death nor sorrow can separate us from the love of God.

I am grateful to those who have freely shared their life stories with me so that others may be helped in working through grief.

I owe a special debt of gratitude to Charlie Gills, pastor of Trinity Lutheran Church, Havertown, Pennsylvania, for his zealous enthusiasm, keen insight, and clear vision. He inspired and assisted me when I needed it most. He also suggested the title of this book from a favorite poem.

—Abraham Schmitt
Souderton, Pennsylvania

Turn Again to Life

How Do You Mend
a Broken Heart?

In England, along a narrow cobblestone street, there is said to be a little fix-it shop where people bring their broken toasters, waffle irons, and lamps for repair. The sign outside the shop contains only four words, but they are among the most hopeful words in the world— *"Nothing Broken Beyond Repair."*

What hopeful, encouraging, soul-nourishing words!

These are hard words to believe, though, when your heart has been overburdened. But after years of counseling the grief-stricken, I believe them. When you read the story of Pastor Craig Landis, you will believe them, too.

Craig Landis comes from a family at high risk for a heart attack. No male in his family has survived past 40 years of age. Knowing this, Craig has lived like a man trying to pack more into a suitcase than it was made to hold. He has continually pressured himself to more intense service in the church, often straining his heart to the limit.

At age 36, Craig had his first bypass surgery. Following a rushed recovery, he threw himself again into the programs of the church where he was pastor. He felt an urgent need to get back to running the church and to keep life under his control. Predictably, he suffered a heart attack.

Craig's diseased heart condition is not what caused his heart to break, however. It was an even deeper hurt. Craig's teenage son Marc was defiant and using drugs. Nothing Craig and his wife, Anne, tried, including professional help, imposing parental limits, even praying for him, made any difference. Their son seemed bent on self-destruction. Only God knows how many small hurts and slights, how many thoughtless words and well-intentioned, but misunderstood, conversations were exchanged.

In one awful, explosive night it happened. Marc and a close friend, Dan, stole away on a night in November. After many "hits" of acid, far more than they had ever taken before, they handcuffed themselves together and leaped over the cliff of a local quarry. Three hundred feet below, their crumpled bodies were found by some friends.

Just prior to their fatal leap, the boys had filled three hours of cassette tape with their own sermon—a running commentary on the last hours of their lives. They recorded a rambling conversation, inspired by excessive use of LSD, including bizarre comments and outbursts. Even worse, the tapes were filled with crude accusations and biting attacks on their parents, contrasted with sentimental good-byes to their girlfriends—a tragic last will and testament of two tormented souls. These bitter tapes weighed heavily on Craig's already overburdened heart!

The local, regional, and even national media picked up the story and had a field day. Every new bit of trivia, every scrap of evidence, anything somebody said, including parents, school officials, or classmates, became headline news.

Marc's dominance in the dual suicide was especially emphasized. It seems that the community needed a villain in the whole affair, and Marc was selected. The Landis parsonage became the lightning rod for this gathering storm of accusations and morbid curiosity.

Things became even worse. Three weeks after Marc's death, his girlfriend, Michelle, tried to take her own life. Other suicides had been hinted, and even attempted. Had Marc's fatal plunge set off an epidemic? Craig and Anne were shaken and preoccupied by this prospect as well, driving them further from the grief process they needed to work through regarding Marc. Craig visited Michelle in the hospital, trying to lift her from her depression.

Michelle brooded over Marc until, a few weeks after her release, she acted in a carefully premeditated way. She drove the new car her parents had bought her to a secluded spot where she and Marc had often met. In a last gesture of defiance, she camouflaged the car with branches and leaves so it couldn't be seen, even from above. Then she ended her life there. In her way of thinking she had joined Marc.

This brought more spotlights to the Landis parsonage, more media coverage, more attempts to blame Marc, and more stress for Craig's breaking heart.

At a time when they should have been grieving the loss of their 17-year-old son, they couldn't. There was no time to grieve. Craig had a second severe heart attack. This time, he was scheduled for sextuple bypass surgery.

Ironically, Craig entered the hospital the day Marc would have celebrated his eighteenth birthday. What a sad legacy Marc had left behind—year after year of heartbreak and pain. Such thoughts were on Craig's mind when a pastor friend called on him. They were good friends, part of a faith community that specializes in helping others with their grief. As it is with good friends, few words were needed. They both knew the depth of the tragedy, but it was up to Craig to articulate it for himself.

Craig, his own life very much in the balance, looked up from the array of tubes and bandages, and quietly asked, "I know that the surgeon has mended my physical heart, but how do you mend a broken heart?"

He had captured it all in one searing question. Grief causes a terrible tearing of the heart. But suicide scatters all the pieces so that mending seems impossible. His heart seemed broken beyond repair.

In the months ahead, God would use a caring coalition of family, many friends, events, and even dreams, to heal that brokenness. God would teach Craig to let go of many things and to learn the price of grief.

Eighteen months after Marc's death, I found myself facing Craig and Anne Landis in their parsonage, next door to the church. This was the same place where all the reporters had badgered them for one more item of sensational information. It seemed unreal. I was nervous. My immediate impression of them was one of wholeness and health.

The moment I sat down I realized that I had taken the exact spot where I had first seen them sitting in a news photo, as if I were literally trying to put myself in their place. That was a comforting thought for me. I looked over at Craig as he took his favorite chair nearby. Even now he had to protect himself because of his most recent surgery, this time for a hernia. His warm, shy smile comforted me.

Anne pulled up a chair. She appeared composed, but later admitted feeling some anxiety in meeting yet another new person who wanted to know their story. She was understandably guarded.

As the conversation began, I quickly realized that I was again permitted to participate in a mending process.

For the first three months after Marc's death, there

had been no time to grieve. When they were not dealing with Michelle's suicide, or Craig's heart attack and
surgery, they were busy fending off the news-hungry
and curious. They had to cope with the barrage of
reporters who demanded a right to the news, without
regard to the Landises' drained condition.

Anne began to tell about their experiences:

*Craig felt the media had hit us in a state of shock.
If he had it to do over again he wouldn't have said
one word to them. The phone rang off the hook with
reporters badgering us for details and information.
Most reporters were not very polite or considerate.
They didn't care at all about the individuals and the
families. They were only concerned with getting the
scoop first and sensationalizing it later.*

*When Michelle attempted suicide the first time,
Craig went to the hospital to see her. The visit affected him very strongly—seeing how withdrawn
and unresponsive she was. How helpless he felt!
Then she succeeded only a few weeks later. Michelle
had been missing for three days so it was really
preying on our minds.*

Both Craig and Anne said, "It is good to talk with
you this way," and I felt their acceptance of me as one
who wanted to help. The simple retelling of their tor-
ment, as well as our later conversations, have eased
their pain a bit more. They have been able to gather
their thoughts, and experience still more mending.

I suggested to Craig and Anne that they begin to
"journal," to record for themselves and relive their
emotions during the time after Marc's death.

People in deep grief sometimes fail to pay attention
to their dream life. Often, these messages from the
soul carry important clues as to what is ailing us.

In his journals, Craig often refers to his dreams. Craig told of the following dream as one that contained a significant message for him.

About two weeks before my first open heart surgery I dreamed that I was in quicksand struggling to get out. In the dream a commentator was on the edge of the swamp videotaping this whole thing for a documentary, to show how the human being—when threatened by death—can put out amazing energy just to survive. He was giving a calm and erudite explanation of my struggle in this quicksand. I was screaming at him for help. He ignored my pleas and kept on waxing eloquent about the psychological and other aspects of surviving when a person is sinking in quicksand. Finally, I cursed him up and down for not listening to me or trying to help me. But it made no difference, he still did not listen! It was then that I decided just to give in and relax, and let whatever happened happen.

The moment I relaxed I started floating to the top. Then I made my way by a breaststroke to the edge of the swamp, where the commentator was waiting. He reached out, pulled me out, and held me tight. Then I woke up.

It was very vivid in my mind, but its meaning was unclear. I was admitted to the hospital for open heart surgery. I was trying to maintain a strong composure and thought I had everything under control.

The night before the surgery they allowed Anne and me to be together. Then she left. I watched her walk to the car. I remembered seeing the taillight of the Vega fading over the hill of route 309. I thought that might be the last time I'd ever see her.

I thought, "Boy, you're struggling for control!" Then, it occurred to me. The dream was a clear message to "stop struggling."

As I was about to go to sleep, I prayed, "Okay, Lord, from now on it's up to you. What happens, happens! I am no longer going to try to control it. It is in your hands."

God was there. I guess the struggle was to accept the whole thing. I prayed, "Help me to accept this and let my life continue as you want it to continue." Support from friends and family was phenomenal. This was the first line of support. They came quickly and continuously. They lined up a guest preacher for me for the next day and for months afterward. Church council members came to comfort and listen, and do whatever was needed.

On the fateful day Anne felt the need to work to relieve her anxiety and the tension of waiting for Marc's death to be confirmed by police, she did laundry and baked cookies all afternoon. A pastor friend helped her bake, and patiently watched us pace back and forth in the kitchen. The bishop came right away and that was helpful too.

Most crucial were the prayers of people and knowing they really cared. Physical touching and hugging was so important.

The lay people took over running the church. They also continued sending us cards and notes. Even for months afterward, certain persons sent me a note or card every week to let me know they cared.

In a suicide, there are so many victims. Craig was reminded how others had suffered when a plant arrived at the parsonage on November 19, the first anniversary of Marc's death. Craig told about the healing he found in this gift from Michelle's parents.

That was the ice breaker with Michelle's parents. Then we felt they cared. Since then we have come to know them as trusted friends through the Survivors of Suicide group. That was important in our own healing—to know that they did not hold a grudge against us. Dan's parents visited us in April. That time of talking and sharing some feelings was another helpful experience in our recovery.

As is often the case where suicides are concerned, the survivors can be a great comfort to each other. Craig also described how his return to pastoral duties helped him.

While I was serving a tour as hospital chaplain, I was summoned to the emergency unit. The nurse asked me to offer a prayer with a family who had just lost a member through sudden death. I did and after the prayer they asked for my name. One woman recognized me as the father of Marc, the boy "everyone had heard about." A peaceful glow covered her face as she expressed gratitude for my presence. There was a deep sense of kinship because she knew I really understood the feelings they were experiencing at that moment. I was no stranger to death. I was needed and valued. I felt that God had given me a special "understanding."

Craig's summer led him to a difficult confrontation with his limiting health problems and the demands of the ministry. He loves the church and the people he serves, but he also loves life.

On my last visit he described a recent experience which shook him and will probably change the course of his ministry:

Reading the announcement of Pastor John Long's death is what really started me thinking. I came home from vacation, opened the mail, and found that this former colleague had suddenly died of a heart attack. John's death was a shock to me. It made me think of my own life and my situation. It's in the back of my mind that the same thing could happen to me. John had a previous heart attack. He knew he had to ease up. But he loved his job and the pressure must have been very high.

I could wind up the same way as John! I don't particularly want to do that because I enjoy being married to Anne and want to stay married as long as I can. I love my work in the church and also want to continue to serve as long as possible.

I have finally become realistic. I know that with my heart I can't expect to live my threescore and sixteen, as the actuarial table says I should. I must take it easier. I've proposed to the church board that we get some kind of help. We had a meeting and they told me of their concerns for my health. They expressed anxiety about how to solve the parish problems and keep me healthy as well. I know I would be of no use to anybody six feet under the ground.

I have thought a lot about dying since Marc's death, and I have come to a conclusion. I cannot say that I am looking forward to death, but I am not as afraid of it as I used to be. When it comes, it comes, and I think I can accept it. I am not so much afraid of dying as I am of going before my time. I know my heart is not going to last forever, but I don't want to push it beyond its potential. In my understanding of the Bible, Moses and others lived to ripe old ages. God granted them longevity because they were in tune with him. I guess I am trying to bring my life into harmony with God's rhythm.

The race, the stress, the driving pressures of my life—all work to keep me out of synch. It will be a major step if I can go into partial retirement. That's the trick of being able to let go. I was struggling in the quicksand again. I have felt that for a while. My personality is such that I like to be in control and have *everything right. I still get upset when I don't have every little detail under control.*

Facing retirement is a grief experience, a smaller "letting go" that I need to face. It's a scary prospect!

I think letting go of these things is a mini-preparation for the "final letting go"—death—when all my control is gone. For me, the important thing is to let go without fear, to let God be in complete control of that final good-bye. All of life is a preparation to say goobye to things and people you have come to love.

Craig Landis is no longer a man struggling in quicksand. He has learned to let go, and is floating out of the quicksand quite nicely. The lesson that Craig Landis can teach us about grief is significant.

Grief can take an enormous toll on the human body. For Craig, this was accentuated by a constitution that was already weakened by hereditary factors. This was complicated by his built-in excessive need to control his destiny. Death wrenched this control away from him and his system paid the price. The nature and number of deaths at an early age in his family were unusually high. His heart literally suffered a breakdown and he was forced to yield to events beyond his control.

In this surrendering process Craig found God very near. Friends, family, and members of the congregation became more precious to him. He also made a deeper commitment to his wife, Anne. Nevertheless he still had to make the difficult journey back—to turn again to life. This happened as he told his story again. Craig's grieving had to be delayed for two years because of a rapid succession of events. When he finally had time, Craig discovered the secret of how to mend a broken heart. Now he is able to show the way to others.

A Tenacious Journey Back

Surely, everyone in the class knew about the deaths of these women's children since their pictures appeared in some of the printed course material. For the first several days they did not identify themselves so as to avoid too much limelight. Then the reporter who wrote about their story appeared as a guest lecturer, and they became central to the class discussion. It seemed that these two women had to step out boldly into the world and make their lives count. To withdraw and hide would have been self-destructive. But did they have to go to this extreme?

The rewards for this venture were significant. Anne told me that she had recently read an earlier book I had written on death and that she now understood my central message: When persons courageously confront the topic of death, they discover a new quality of life. Anne noticed this happen to other fellow graduate students. Dialoguing with death is really contagious.

Many would assume that a concentrated summer course on suicide would be a most morbid experience. The exact opposite was true. Anne's demeanor proved it. She was beaming with radiant life.

After I left, something phenomenal occurred. Through dealing with me around this manuscript, switches were turned on within her. More grief and healing was still needed. In a note to me, Anne wrote:

I have been walking around in a daze trying to recover from this overwhelming experience at the sui-

cide workshop. I feel disoriented and frustrated. It seems like I have a lot of emotions within me which can't get out.

Reading your book Dialogue with Death [out of print] and speaking with you today, on top of this past week's experience, has led me to several unexpected struggles.

After you left I sat down and read and reread the manuscript, penciled in my comments, and stopped where you spoke about "the day Marc left home. . . ." I began to feel the urge to write down more specifically my feelings about his life and death.

The day Marc left home in July, we didn't know where he went. We had a very uneasy feeling, as he left us a subtle suicide message on a "Black Sabbath" tape and told us he wouldn't be around to bug us anymore.

Marc was a very ambiguous person. He was an affectionate child, but a brooder. He had many friends, yet he was a fiercely independent thinker. He had a real soft spot for defenseless people and animals, but as he grew older he could be vicious and cruel. He created beauty with lines. His detailed drawings were painstakingly drawn in pen and ink from the time he started school, but he never corrected or fixed anything. He had a short fuse, and would destroy things the instant they didn't work perfectly. His subjects were superheroes and monsters waging war with Satan. His choice of music was acid rock. His own body became grotesque in his drawings as it was gradually distorted and destroyed by drugs. Despite the admiration of peers and praise of family, Marc recognized neither his own talents nor his worth as a person. He ended up destroying himself.

Marc went through many years of lashing out and blaming others for his life. I think at the end he realized the choices were really his, and he couldn't live with his choice. I think he felt change was im-

*possible and he had no hope for the future. He left
many clues to these thoughts and feelings in his
writings and drawings.*

*If I said I didn't feel any guilt, I would be both a
fool and a liar. I learned to parent by trial and error
and made many errors, I am sure, for which I will always feel some guilt. I often replay them in my
"mind's eye"—rehearsing how I might have acted out
my role differently in this or that circumstance. This
is a painful exercise in futility.*

*Here is my own ambiguity: In the end I am left
with a strong awareness that I was not the best
mother to this very special child. But yet I also truly
believe I did the best I could. Marc made choices for
himself which I could not control. In the struggle I
learned to let go. I recall my own childhood as a
"struggle for self." I grew out of it stubborn and te-
nacious toward life. Marc, for whatever reason, was
not enough of a fighter and could not survive the
struggle.*

*It is hard to grieve for a suicide. How can I, a
mother, accept that the fragile life I nurtured and
protected has rejected my love and guidance? I feel
like an artist who has just spent hours and hours
creating a beautiful picture only to have someone
grab it from my hands and tear it up. Although I prac-
ticed and raced hard for years, I have been disqualified as a mother at the finish line! My pain is all
mixed up with feelings of rejection.*

*It's hard to grieve for a suicide. My feelings of loss
are entangled with knots of anger. I have such sadness that my son will never be able to accept people's
love, to feel valued as a person, to touch other lives, to
have the satisfaction of an accomplished goal, or to
surround me with grandchildren. But at the same
time, I am so angry for the years of hostility and
cruelty he gave us, the anxiety and stress he brought
to our family life and the pain he has inflicted on us*

all by his death. Yet his death has also relieved my anguish and his own inner pain. I relive the jump off the cliff, the smashing of his body, the pain and then nothing. [Marc and a close friend had handcuffed themselves together and jumped from a cliff in a local quarry.]

I imagine he is free from his struggle. I felt this relief most strongly last summer when I was walking alone on the beach, watching the ocean currents and the seagulls above. These intense and conflicting feelings of sadness, anger, and relief wash over me in waves, day after day, with a strange confusion. My heart is broken. It does daily battle and drains my energy. Often, though, an automatic plastic shield of numbness covers all the feelings and allows me to function quite well. I may be clumsy and forgetful one moment, and insanely hysterical with laughter the next; anxious, jumpy, and bitchy one day; dull, lethargic, and useless the next.

Healing does come, slowly, with the support of my circle of family and friends, a job I enjoy, humor, daily physical exercise, and faith in God. But I have been changed forever and my life will never be the same. I hold on more tightly to the moments I love, but it becomes easier to let go. In having control wrenched from my life by a suicide, I have learned a little more to give up control and to trust in God's guidance and strength. It has deepened my respect and tolerance for others and has led me to immerse myself in their struggles. We are all connected! . . . Once we get into grieving it has a way of taking us back into some very old experiences. It is like a "feeling flashback." Things just come tumbling out that we haven't thought about in years. . . . "

Twenty-two years ago our daughter Beth, our first child, was born with my husband of one year looking on. I knew something was wrong by the way the doctor and attendants scurried around in silence and by *the blue color of her skin. Later, I was told she was a Down's Syndrome baby and was mentally re-tarded—I should not get close to her or learn to love her, but place her in an institution immediately. Thus, they thought I would be protected, would not feel the loss of a child or need to suffer grief. How wrong they were!*

Back in my private room, they placed me in an antiseptic bed and sent my meals on a tray. I felt like a misfit, a prisoner. I saw other mothers' babies wheeled in for feedings; photographer fathers trying to catch just the right moment; heard the infant wails of hunger, and the proud praises of aunts and uncles and grandparents. But for me, shut away in my silent room, there was only the pain of isolation.

My parents brought flowers—blue flag iris and spring daffodils, each blossom in its perfect beauty and clear color accenting the imperfections of the child I was not permitted to see or hold or hear or feed. My husband brought sad eyes and kind words and his love, trying to break the news softly to shield me from the pain.

On the third or fourth day, drowning in waves of unasked questions, unexpressed anger and unre-lieved pain, I let out my silent screams for the first time, venting all of my grief upon a pink-skirted maid who was mopping the floor around my bed. While other staff had meticulously avoided my room and performed all necessary tasks with perfunctory effi-ciency, she alone cared for me with a warm smile and friendly chatter. How embarrassing it was for me to lose it all and make a scene! I can laugh at it now because it certainly got results.

My family was notified of my hysteria. Nurses came running. My doctor was called. Finally, some-body asked me what I needed. I wanted to hold my baby! I was a mother who didn't feel like a mother. After a few hours of labor, my swollen abdomen had collapsed and suddenly returned to near normal size. The physical signs of motherhood were gone with nothing to show for it!

Finally that evening, led by my husband, the pediatrician appeared with Beth in his arms, looking sad and ill-at-ease with the task he had undertaken—introducing a distraught mother to the unfinished child he was holding.

Maintaining his professional distance, he explained Beth's mind would always be childlike and never mature. He demonstrated the physical signs of Down's—separation of toes, lack of nose bridge, thick tongue, floppy limbs and head, and generally poor muscle tone. He said she hadn't yet developed a sucking reflex and needed to be taught this by stimulation. He suggested that we place Beth in an institution right from the hospital because surely we could not deal with the difficulties of her care for life. I held her and felt like a mother for the first time. It was a tearful and awesome feeling.

The rest is "history." Craig and I were both full-time students. Graduation for me was six weeks away. We needed time to process all that had happened: to adjust to our first year of marriage, to grieve for our child who could never grow up, and to finish the old business of my education. Fortunately we received good advice. We placed Beth in a temporary church-sponsored foster home for three months. After several nervous visits, supportive encouragement of family and friends, and many times of sharing talk and tears, we made the decision to bring Beth home and raise her to whatever potential she possessed.

It has been both a struggle and a blessing to have Beth with us. I can't think of any experience which forced me to struggle or grow more during the early years of our marriage. Beth has completed her education. She can read, count money, do the dishes, fold her laundry, and pack her own lunch every day.

She calls friends on the phone and gets a paycheck every week from her sheltered workshop where she has a job from 9:00-4:00. She has an active social life with her own peers and even does volunteer work at a nursing home. She has earned self-respect. God has given me the courage to grieve and the strength to grow.

Many persons would have assumed that these events were the punishment of God. Others might have ruled out God totally and become atheists. Many rational minds cannot comprehend it any other way, but Anne and her husband, Craig, were able to find meaning and hope even after such tragedy.

Here is Anne's view:

I don't believe in predestination. I think God puts us here, puts his Spirit in us, and gives us the freedom to make decisions and choices in our lives. The choices we make, combined with circumstances beyond our control, determine who we are and chart our direction in life.

I don't think God deliberately gives us any particular trial. I think life takes care of that nicely. God allows us to struggle with it and says, "Here I am! This is what I offer you." And we have to respond to that—learn how to survive through the struggles that we have, which just naturally occur. I think this is part of everybody's life. It's just a matter of degree, or the weight you put to it. People have said to us, "How can you deal with one more thing? It isn't fair. You've had so much happen to you."

But for us it's all relative. You feel at the time that it's far too much to bear, but then you hear other people's stories and you think "Oh, this is life." Life is a struggle! That is the message M. Scott Peck conveys in his book The Road Less Traveled.

The theme of the book is that life is difficult and a struggle, and what we make of our lives is how we struggle with the difficulties. It's not that we're born to be happy or that we shouldn't have to struggle, or that there is something blemished in our character if we have all these horrible events happen to us. It is how we face the struggles that determines who we are.

While the dream carried Craig through the first operation, The Road Less Traveled *helped him survive Marc's suicide and his next open heart operation. Craig explains it this way:*

"I would like to believe that the hand of God was in all this. Anne's Aunt Mary came across this book and thought we should read it. About a month before Marc took his life, the book arrived, so I started reading it. It was a perfect preparation for what was ahead! God does not protect us from crises and struggles, but he provides the means to overcome them."

Anne knew the model for grieving intuitively, long before I showed her academically. Anne knew that she had to go back over the whole span of her son's and daughter's lives repeatedly. This came to her naturally—almost like the easy swing of the pendulum of an old grandfather's clock. At the same time she does not do this just for the sake of doing it. She chooses her time carefully, or she capitalizes on the opportunities that come her way. After each swing back and forth, she returns to the present with more strength, more will to live, and more hope for the future.

The most significant return journey I am aware of was the one she shared with me. I had learned a lot about the family's disaster through following the news releases. This made me reluctant to approach her, since I did not want to become another media event. I did not want to become part of the problem, but I hoped to contribute to her healing. Two years after the death, she was ready to walk with me through her autobiography of grief.

It was not sufficient for Anne to tell her story to me. She needed to write it. After each visit, entire scenarios played back for her, so she picked up her pen and wrote profusely. Precise details could not be forgotten; they had to be noted and kept for posterity. I was permitted to share this material, if I so desired. If not, it was worth writing just for its healing effect. Anne used journaling to capitalize on the crucial moments of living with Marc, the loss of Marc, and life following Marc's death.

Anne fought tenaciously to find her place during the early years. Now she fought just as tenaciously to grieve, so that she could live again. She was aware that she had to live a different life—not a simple continuation of the old life. Marc's death had been a huge interruption, and her life after his death was disinctively different. She anticipated that, so she could embrace it even though she had not chosen it. The hallmark of healthy grieving is openness to the future regardless of what the future holds.

Then Anne chose to make another major journey back. She enrolled in a class on suicide—where her story would be the central drama. Sometimes one must do the unusual in order to make peace with the past. When a death is catastrophic, heroic efforts are needed to live again.

One of the most moving aspects of this experience with Anne was her return to an earlier grief. Since we were already on a healing journey, why not go back to the time before Marc was born and examine another wound? She had experienced grief when her first child was born with Down's Syndrome. The real pain was caused by the physician and the hospital staff who treated the child as a disposable object. Beth was Anne's baby, regardless of the genetic error. Anne had carried Beth for nine months, loved her in anticipation, and she needed to be bonded to her. That scene had to be revisited. Now she was ready to be honest about her feelings, explore them, tell them, and then let go of them. Another major wound had been healed.

Anne keeps saying it's hard to grieve for a suicide, while at the same time she is showing us how to grieve. I agree it's hard. That means more courage is needed to do it.

Thanks, Anne, for inviting me to walk with you. I experienced renewal as you found healing and showed us all how to grieve.

The Emotional Phases
of Grief

Grief takes a heavy toll on those who remain behind. We have known this for a long time. More recently research has verified what we knew intuitively. In a report on the causes of 1,300 deaths in London in the year 1657, one physician observed that 10 were caused by grief. One might question how he arrived at that conclusion. He must have known that these deaths followed other deaths, and there was just cause for that diagnosis.

Recently, a well-documented study showed that the death rate among 4,486 widowers past the age of 54 was almost 40 percent higher than average during the first six months after the loss of their wives. Three quarters of them died from heart disease. The most common cause of death was coronary thrombosis. One conclusion is that acute grief is hazardous to the survivors.

The question that remains is, What does it take to choose to live after a loss that has taken a severe toll on the bereaved?

One of the best ways to identify the ways that grief takes its toll is to read C. S. Lewis's book *A Grief Observed.* His motive was not to write a book; he only used a journal to come to terms with the loss of his wife. At one point in writing he decided to stop journaling, lest he get carried away with it and never end. Grief had a way of engulfing him every day; so there was an endless flow of material. One might even speculate whether this loss did not contribute to his own death. I gather that he wrote the journal immediately after the death of his wife. It was published when he was 63, and he died two years later.

"No one ever told me that grief felt so like fear," he writes. "I am not afraid, but the sensation is like being afraid. The same fluttering in the stomach, the same restlessness, the yawning. I keep swallowing.

"An odd by-product of my loss is that I'm aware of being an embarrassment to everyone I meet. At work, at the club, in the street, I see people, as they approach me, trying to make up their minds whether they'll 'say something about it' or not. I hate it if they do, and if they don't.

"To some, I'm worse than an embarrassment. I am a death's head. Whenever I meet a happily married pair I can feel them both thinking, 'One or the other of us must someday be as he is now.' "

This is what grief is all about and much more. The emotions keep erupting—and at the most unexpected times. Often these emotions are so new and unfamiliar that grieving persons will not dare share them even with closest friends for fear that they will be labeled bizarre. This fear then drives them to greater isolation and pain. C. S. Lewis describes this process also and wonders if he is condemned to bear it forever.

Is it any wonder that it takes courage to grieve? But who wants to be courageous when they are hurting? For once a person should have the right to be a coward and collapse. This is permissible periodically. A grieving person should be given the right to retreat in bed, curled up in cowardice. However, that cannot be for long, lest one get trapped by the relief and never rise to face the world again.

In detailing the emotional phases of the dying process, Elisabeth Kübler-Ross made a great contribution to understanding the grief process. This was not her intention, nor was it even her conclusion. What she did was interact with dying persons until she deciphered the phases that are common to the dying experience. The names and order of these phases were not as important as the fact that she gave dying patients the right to feel their emotions. This gave friends and relatives the same right. Her greatest contribution was that dying persons and their kin could understand each other and then together experience the final stage of growth. This was in direct contrast to earlier practices when the final stage was torture as both parties wove a web of deceit until death mercifully rescued them from each other.

Next came the major serendipitous gift of Dr. Kübler-Ross. Those who were left behind discovered that not only did dying persons go through these phases, but the grieving ones also experienced them. Death had brought the one process to an end, but it had also started a new one. Thus, the Kübler-Ross model became a guide for grief also.

The resolution of loss does not mean that a person forgets the deceased or that at a most unexpected moment one may not be overcome with intense emotions. It is more appropriate to say that the grief work is complete when the person can comfortably and realistically remember the one who has gone. This means that the good and the bad, the pleasures and disappointments, of the past relationship are evenly balanced. Then a person is able to continue his or her own life in the absence of the deceased.

Upon hearing about a death, the first reaction is *shock*. The news of a death is often too much for one's nervous system to bear, so a merciful switch simply turns it off. This is the human psyche's automatic circuit-breaker. In this state, the mind often goes into automatic pilot. These persons may calmly go about the work that must be done showing no feelings. Some people have been known to remove all the tubes, close the eyes, and even give the body a kiss as if it were routine.

This phase has limited value. Life demands that a person come out of shock and engage in living. Then another protective gimmick switches on—*denial.* It is as if the unconscious is saying to the person, "This is not really happening to me." While in Nazi concentration camp, Bruno Bettelheim discovered that his system used denial to survive his incredible lot. He felt that he was standing at a distance watching the atrocities happen. At times it seemed as if he were reading a novel or watching a movie about himself.

Denial permits time to pass until more appropriate mechanisms can be employed. Whenever any mechanism is not doing its job or the person is between stages, denial increases to fill the void.

When denial no longer works, *anger* is the first conscious mechanism used. It is as if the person is forced to admit that the loss occurred, but then must retaliate negatively. "If me, then why me?" The anger may be directed at anyone or everyone; it may be realistic or unrealistic. People often find a "villain" upon whom to place the responsibility for the death. Medical personnel or facilities are frequently the target. Grieving persons are vulnerable and open to suggestions for lawsuits. Apparently it is more comforting to strike out at an identifiable villain than to move on in the grief process.

These three emotional phases—*shock, denial,* and

anger—make up the first third of the grief journey. They all involve *rejecting the fact of the loss.* Then the person moves to the second third of the resolution process—*reconciliation with the loss.* This requires that a person begin to engage the reality that the loved one is gone.

Bargaining is the first step in engaging this process. "If only I had the loved one back, I would do everything I should have done and nothing I should not have done." In loss, bargaining is a smaller issue than in the dying process. A greater amount of bargaining may be present in fantasy. This is when the grieving person brings the lost one back by daydreaming and thereby creates another ending. This is a short-lived stage because it is not fruitful. It also may be used as a delaying tactic because the next phase is the real trial by fire.

The next emotional phase usually is called "depression and preparatory grief." I prefer to call it *depression and preparation for acceptance.* When all the previous stages are of no real help, out of sheer helplessness a person sinks into despair. Depression is a way of creating distance from other people and crawling into oneself to be alone. Resolutions begin, not in the outer world, but in the inner world. While psychologically cut off from the outer world, a person finally comes face-to-face with oneself. Then the individual gains the strength to say, "Okay, my loved one is gone forever. So who am I now? Where am I going?"

At the moment a person can ask those questions from the depth of the heart, one can enter the final stage of grief—yielding to the loss. When an emotional *acceptance* emerges, the person is ready to continue living without the deceased.

The original work of Dr. Kübler-Ross defined another stage—decathexis. This means that a person withdraws all feelings and becomes tranquil and ready to die. It seems an inappropriate stage for the grieving model since there should be times in the years after a loss that a person is fully at peace about the death. At this time the survivor would not have a need to withdraw any longer.

Clearly there will be intense emotions in grieving persons. These may follow in a sequence, can be understood, and are appropriate. However, merely contemplating the stages may evoke emotions. Who wants to go through all that—especially when the choice was not one's own? It was decided by another's death. Again, this calls for fortitude to live this mortal life.

Lest one feel that the grieving process always is neat and orderly, there is another perspective. In real life, nothing is this nicely organized. C. S. Lewis, grappling with his own grieving, did not have the luxury of theorizing in an armchair: "An admirable programme," he wrote. "Unfortunately it can't be carried out. Tonight all hells of young grief have opened again; the mad words, the bitter resentment, the fluttering in the stomach, the nightmare unreality, the wallowed-in tears. For in grief nothing 'stays put.' One keeps on emerging from a phase, but it always recurs. Round and round. Everything repeats. Am I going in circles, or dare I hope I am on a spiral? But if a spiral, am I going up or down it?"

What, then, is courage in grief? Courage in grief is the decision to live again—to turn again to life—when one has all the excuses and evidence necessary never to try again. To live again is to form new relationships, but that only makes one vulnerable to another loss. Then the person may be devastated another time. So why try? Why not give up? To live again is to move into the future and face a whole new set of unknowns, with no guarantee that another death will not occur.

To choose to live again in the face of all this means to move ahead in spite of the risk. Healthy grief is to choose to relive the tragic loss in such a way as to eventually let go of that person and move on to new relationships. One does this with the poignant awareness that all future relationships are just as fragile as the one just ended. This decision takes courage.

The reward for trying again is discovering that every tragedy has the potential for transformation. It may even mean that life after the loss has a quality that far exceeds the previous life. It is the discovery that deep intimacies are experienced between persons who have been through deep valleys of despair. Sharing can be of a quality they might never have known had they not mutually experienced losses. Even to desire to experience this renewed life takes courage.

Finally, for a few courageous ones, there is an opportunity to learn from death and complete the mission for the deceased. Creative courage can take patterns of an old life, reshuffle them, and bring new meaning to others and oneself that would never have been accomplished in an uninterrupted life.

Surely, someone who has lost a loved one has earned the right to be a coward. However, to continue on that path will result only in another victim. To stand up against all odds is the most courageous choice. It is the only way to begin to live again.

The death of a loved one means that life for the survivors changes directions. They are forced to take a new road that they did not choose. At times it is a road they never would have wanted to travel. The courage in grief is to be able to take this road and pay the price until a new life emerges in the absence of the deceased.

Choosing to Live Again

In April, just before Martha and Jerome Troyer were scheduled to celebrate their forty-fifth wedding anniversary, Martha began to suffer severe pains in her abdomen. She suspected cancer. Her physician also anticipated something serious. So she began making preparations to die. Instead, two months later her husband died and she recovered.

I was certain I had cancer when I was ill, because of the kind of pain that I had. I was not going to let anyone know, because I knew this anniversary celebration was coming up and I wanted it to be a happy time. And it was!

The reason I could be so happy was that I had read the book My Glimpse of Eternity, *by Betty Maltz, who was pronounced dead for twenty minutes. She told how her spirit floated up to heaven and came back into her body. I was just thinking how enjoyable it would be to go to heaven.*

Jerome and I talked a lot about my death, and I told him that I didn't want him to stay in our home alone. I felt that he would be too lonely and would be unable to handle the house and the yard. He needed to be with people and became restless if he had a day off from work and was alone at home. I suggested that he might go to Greencroft Retirement Center, where he could be near other people.

Then one evening when I was working through this, some people came to sell us a tombstone. They had seen our anniversary picture in the paper. I was very upset that those people came. At this point I was working through death, and I thought, "I don't want to see or think about a tombstone." I just wanted those people to leave. But my husband continued talking to them. We ended up buying a tombstone. Tombstones seemed to have nothing to do with the emotional process of dying, and I was not ready to face tombstones at that point.

I was determined to wait to see the doctor until after the anniversary because I didn't want the children and my husband to be apprehensive. I thought it was malignant because I had excruciating pain and I'd heard that this is the way cancer works.

I felt I could work through this myself and we could just be a happy family together for the celebration. Then, before the children who lived out of state left, I shared with them that I thought I had cancer.

I told my husband that evening. Jerome mentioned something about a spot that hurt when he tried to lie on his right side. So I told him to have it checked to see if it was anything serious.

Then I made an appointment with the doctor and went in to his office within several days. They ran me through a lot of tests. They also started running tests on him and they put me on hold. He had emphysema as a result of his welding shop work and his lungs started filling up, so they hospitalized him. At this time he was in for fifteen days. After he returned home, he was still very weak, but the doctor told me, "Now it's time for you to go in." I told him I was afraid he would say that.

They operated on me and found that it was a broken blood vessel that gave me a lot of pain because the blood had collected and clotted. They said they had never seen anything like that before.

When I came out of the recovery room, I don't recall that anyone told me that it was not malignant. When I was back in my room, I heard a couple of my daughters whispering, "Oh, I'm so glad Mom doesn't have cancer." Then I thought, "Wait a minute here! I was ready to die! Jerome's got cancer and he's going to die, and I am not." I thought that if I had cancer, neither of us would need to be alone very long. We'd both be gone and that would be it. I got depressed because I was so ready to die. I never thought I'd get to that place, but that's where I was. I just wanted to die. I thought that would be such a happy time—just to float up to heaven and spend the rest of my life there. It was depressing for me to process this, but I knew that I had to collect myself and take care of Jerome to make these last days as good as I could.

Five days after surgery I returned home but had no time to recover. Jerome was weakening, and I started to take care of him. He regressed so rapidly that it was difficult.

When he was dying, I thought a lot about his going and my staying. I thought "There he goes. He's got peace. He's with Jesus. And here I am." I still think about it once in a while but not as strongly. When I said to my youngest daughter while I was still in the hospital that I wanted to die, she said, "But Mom, God's got something here for you and I don't know if I could have handled it if you had both gone at once."

I realized that I had to discover that I was here for a purpose. When people ask me what I am doing, I tell them what I'm doing and I say I know the Lord has a purpose here for me. I'm going to live to try and find and fulfill that purpose. But I'm not sure that I know exactly what it's all about.

It gets lonely being alone, but then I have really good times too. To get together and just to be with people is one of these.

I did a lot of praying and I opened myself to the Lord and asked him to search me and said, "How do I make this shift [from dying to living]?" It was like a change of direction. I was going down this road and suddenly I had to go back and take another road. It's not nearly as joyful as preparing to die once you are ready to go. Sometimes it seems like a dream that I made that change, and I don't know how I did it. But it was a time of real searching to try and find out.

I did a lot of reading. I read Scripture and books just trying to find out. I just really depended on the Lord a lot to find out and to help me make that change. I guess I've never been so close to the Lord as I was during that time, because I had to take a different route than I had planned. It is difficult to explain.

There were a lot of things through that time that I cannot find words to express. It just seemed like a real disappointment to me. But I also felt that since I'm a Christian I knew the Lord was leading me and he could have just as well taken me on that road. Now I needed to back up and look at life and say, "It's okay! It's all right, Lord. I'm here for a purpose."

So I just moved along day by day. People used to say, "Now how are you doing?" I'd say, "I live each day at a time." At that time I didn't plan ahead. Each day I'd say, "Lord, this is another day and we'll work through it together."

There were times when I planned to visit my daughter in Minnesota or my daughter in Pennsylvania, but in my daily routine it was very much one day at a time.

At that time I was a church elder too, and it seemed that people didn't want to overload me, so they backed off, which was painful. It was another thing to work through. Just day by day, I would go.

I had to reorient myself all over again. It is interesting to me now to see how the Lord took me through my preparation to die so as to prepare me for Jerome's death. It made his death easier for me. It made talking about death a time when I wanted to rejoice. We did talk about death. All of our souls were rejoicing in songs.

*We knew exactly how to prepare for the funeral
and the funeral sermon was uplifting. That's how Jerome would have wanted it. He wouldn't have
wanted it any other way. He had said once that he
was so ready to die. He said, "I just wonder what the
end is going to be like." And I said, "Well, that's something we don't know." It could have gone many different ways, because his death was not caused by
his cancer. If it had been caused by cancer, he might
have lived and suffered many months, if not years.
Death was caused by pneumonia due to the emphysema and it weakened his lungs. He had tuber-
culosis when he was a young child and his lungs
were weak. So he ended up with pneumonia, and we
were so thankful for that. Otherwise, he would have
had much more suffering that would have lasted
longer. It was only six weeks from the time of diagnosis until death.*

Martha's story raises a question that needs to be
addressed. Exactly how does one deal with the order in
which deaths occur? We assume that the oldest generation will die first. Then, as the next moves into
place, it is their turn to die. We comfort ourselves by
believing that as long as we have parents or grandparents living, then we are sheltered from death. We
use our elders to deny the possibility of our death.

But for Martha the order was all mixed up. She had
been bombarded by death from all sides. In her immediate family, while yet in her early forties, her son
died just a week before he was scheduled to be married. She says that her husband and she had a new
experience with the Lord following the death of their
son. Their relationship to God took on more signifi-
cance, and they became closer to the Lord.

Then she lost her young grandson and her mother

in the same year. She had a huge collision with death when three members of her family, involving one generation above her and two generations below her, died within less than two years. Several years later her father also died.

Finally, all the signs indicated that she was next. After she had gone through the enormous emotional phases of dying, including accepting her own death, she discovered these were false signals. Instead, her husband died. Now she found herself in the mid-sixties, with the generations before her gone and members of two generations following her also gone. Living alone, she wondered what this really meant.

A more crucial question that Martha faced was, How could she choose to live again when she had accepted that she was about to die? She said it was like taking death off the shelf and dealing with it. Then she had to put it back on the shelf and go through the process of choosing to live. Regardless of how ready she was to die, this readiness had to be laid aside. In spite of the painful process of yielding to death, she could not remain yielded.

Martha knows that someday she will need to face death again. She will have to repeat the entire painful process. Then she must take death off the shelf once more, and psychologically she must pay the price yet another time.

The message of Martha's experience is that one cannot actively prepare to live and die at the same time. It must be either one or the other. If the appointment with death is canceled, then an apppointment with life must be made again. At that time making the appointment with life proved to be difficult.

Martha's experience yields some interesting insight as we look at the levels of encounter with death described in chapter 5. It is difficult to envision a greater collision with death than Martha experienced. Not only had several of Martha's descendants died, but both her husband and she assumed that she was terminally ill. Hand-in-hand Martha and husband were boldly and bravely walking up to the golden gate prepared to meet their Maker. There could be no denial present; the symptoms were too obvious. Nor could they stop with mere conversations about death and dying. It was not a vicarious experience—no longer an "as if we were dying" dialogue. It was an actual encounter—a straightforward lengthy collision with death.

While this drama was taking place, they moved along together rejoicing. They had spent a lifetime believing that this world was not their home, and that they were just passing through—the words of a familiar song. They were prepared to meet their Savior and Lord at the end of the journey.

Then there was a surprise ending to the final scene in the drama of life. Jerome died and Martha recovered. Now Martha is walking the remainder of the way alone, and she is lonely. She never anticipated being a widow.

As I visited her in her rural Indiana home, I had the distinct feeling that there was some unfinished grieving. It was not hard to notice which had been Jerome's favorite chair. It still was in the same spot as if awaiting his return. The whole house left the impression that it was meant for two people, not for one to live in alone.

Looking out the front window, Martha could see the shop where Jerome had worked—where he had spent so many hours welding. Both Martha and Jerome must have been comforted knowing that they were never far away from each other, unaware that the fumes from the welding torch were slowly taking a toll. This damage shortened Jerome's dying process. In a way Martha was relieved by this, because she knew that a slow death from cancer would have been extremely difficult for her husband.

As we sat quietly at her kitchen table, together we recalled the life that Jerome had once lived here. Martha had taken this journey back many times. She told it with ease to anyone who was interested.

The catch in these journeys back, spanning their 45 years of marriage, is that it wasn't supposed to have ended this way. They really were prepared to enter their final home together. This shift is what makes Martha's grief so difficult. Although she went through all the phases of grief frequently and with ease, I have the impression that there is a degree of shock that remains with her. Or, perhaps a part of Martha really went to heaven with Jerome. A faraway look on her face indicates a focus on her heavenly home; only superficial business remains to be done here on earth, biding the time until she can join her Jerome.

Preparing for Death and Loss

The best preparation for death is to live life deliberately and fully. This means deciding how to live and then doing it. To choose life more completely, one also must choose to face death. To accept the fact that life must end is basic to living life fully now.

I must deal with death. I cannot let go of the subject. I must pursue it over and over again. Death has a secret about living, and I must find it. And when I do, I hope to help others discover this secret also.

Behind this search there is a real desire to make life as meaningful as possible for myself and others. I have a haunting notion that too many people live on too shallow a level. They miss the real joy of living. There is a depth of meaning to life that eludes them. If only people would permit themselves to face their limited life span, they would be forced to make the most of every moment. If we really faced the fact that life will end, would we not live better and with deeper meaning? Would we not make each finite moment count? There is no escape from death, but in this modern era people do all they can to avoid death, to delay it, and to evade all thoughts and conversations about it. Like the subject of sex in former generations, it is taboo.

The most tragic result of denying death is that, in doing this, persons also forfeit life; for death is an essential aspect of the mystery that we call life. It is merely the end of finite existence. To live life fully, one must yield to the limits that this finiteness imposes. But there is another side. To embrace our finiteness opens us to new dimensions of life, for someone has said, "Life is not genuinely our own until we can renounce it."

People often ask, "How can you continue this preoccupation with death? Isn't it morbid?" Far from it. In fact, dealing with death may become a gateway to a new land that often takes on Edenic attributes.

Yes, there are times when I feel as though I have no desire to become further involved in the subject of death. But each time I hear another's story and share the sorrow and struggle, the reward for having risked again far outweighs the cost. To free people to face their worst fears and then in gratitude to infect others with a newly won freedom is a contagious process.

When conducting workshops on death and dying, I frequently use a model to conceptualize the primary message that I wish to convey. I want people to permit themselves to have an intimate collision with finiteness and death in order to live fully. I illustrate this by a series of concentric circles (see diagram on page 52).

Each circle represents a level of involvement with death. The outer circle is the most casual or remote encounter, and the inner circle represents the actual experience of one's own death.

This model can help one visualize the phases in moving from the outermost level to the succeeding ones in order to get as close to the center as possible. It is obvious that few persons really experience dying and then come away to talk about it. We know this is not possible or probable for most of us. The goal is to attempt to die vicariously or to participate so intimately with another's death that you will permit yourself to join a dying person in the experience as deeply as you can.

I assume that there is a progression in difficulty for

individuals or groups to move from the outer level toward the center. Either we innately are not designed to do this, or we are taught not to do it. It might even be that life and death are so opposite to each other that an individual must concentrate on one or the other. However, I contend that there is great merit in pursuing death, even if it is at odds with living. Then one may return to living as a richer person.

Most persons remain at the denial stage all of their

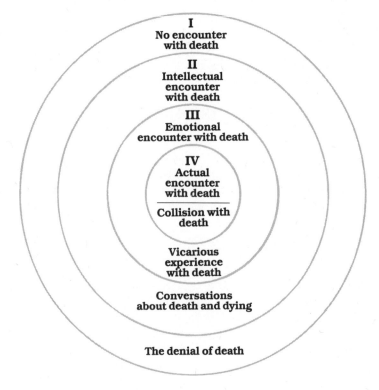

Levels of Encounter with Death

lives. Many want to live as if life will never end. In deal-ing with groups, I find resistance to move beyond this level even though they have enrolled for that exact experience. However, to remain at this outer level creates a penalty. To not face the end of life means that one forfeits a deep encounter with living.

To really claim ownership of your life, you must claim the place in the life cycle where you are pres-ently. It is necessary to recognize that a certain number of years have passed and can never be relived. To accept fully the signs and limitations of any stage is a vital sign of living an emotionally healthy life.

One of the greatest cultural tragedies that has emerged recently is the male midlife crisis. The most significant attribute of this is the bold defiance of the aging process. It is as if these men take a good look ahead, perceive the top of the hill a short distance away, and assume that after that life is all downhill. If they keep on doing whatever they assigned for them-selves to achieve, they will not reach their goals; so they throw away the life script and assume they can begin again with a new script. They deny that they are aging in spite of everything. The result is an enormous disruption to those near them as they disown the life-and-death process while time ticks away as always. An alternative would be to enter level two and begin to reflect on dying, or at least begin conversing about death in philosophical, theological, or rational terms.

We are moving beyond the taboo stage. Death has become a popular topic on television talk shows. It is common to have classes and workshops on death and dying. Most denominations have commissions work-ing to provide additional teaching material and to help congregations who want teaching guides. The subject has been opened to the extent that persons are able to respond to dying and grieving persons rather than re-coiling in fear.

Most individuals have arrived at the point of talking about death and dying, but this is where they stop. Classes may pursue nonthreatening subjects such as the legal definition of death, the Christian's account-ability for making a will, or the meaning of a living will. Areas such as organ transplants, choosing or not choosing kidney dialysis, or perhaps active versus passive euthanasia may also be included. These are valid areas to pursue, but they may be used to avoid a real emotional collision with death.

The desperate need is for persons to permit them-selves to experience vicariously their own death—level three—even as they participate in another's death. Those who enter this phase begin living life anew. They also experience a foretaste of their own death, which inevitably will come later. They are prepared to respond to others close to them who may be dying. They are free to step toward the dying instead of away from them. And if they should suddenly have to deal with a tragic loss, they are better prepared to survive this in a wholesome way.

Few individuals voluntarily move to level four, an actual encounter or collision with death. When death comes to most families, they are at a loss to know what to do or how to feel. It is sad that they are unprepared to participate in this final stage of spiritual growth.

People live poorly because they deal with death poorly. When they must come near the dying, they also respond poorly. If it is their own death, they die poorly and leave survivors who grieve poorly. And the sur-vivors continue the process of living poorly. The sur-vivors may even die earlier because of this cycle. The net result is that the rich reward of dealing with death is lost, and this impoverished cycle is perpetuated generation after generation. The bottom line is that much of the quality of living is lost.

A dear friend of mine in a distant state suffered a critical heart attack at midlife. I was able to monitor his progress through a mutual friend. I yearned to talk to him, but distance prevented this. The reports on him were negative for a long time. The problem did not end with a heart attack. A series of complications followed. Each of these could have been terminal. Months passed as slowly the news became more positive and finally he was declared recovered.

In an attempt to cope with the possibility of his death, I often thought of what such a loss would mean to me. The fact that I could not meet him increased my need to prepare myself for his death. So I grieved deeply.

When I eventually met him, I was intense with my affirmation of his excellent recovery. However, he did not enter into my exuberance. He stared into the distance and gave me nonverbal messages that he did not care to talk about the experience.

I decided to check my information about the seriousness of his illness. Was I wrong in assuming that he was hovering near death for many weeks and that the medical report had given little hope for his survival? His comment was, "Yes, that information could all be correct, but I never gave it a thought that I was dying. I had the full confidence that I would beat it." This was said with a tone of finality that also told me to drop the subject.

Within, I could not drop the subject. I merely told myself that here was a person who was at death's door for an extended period of time who was still denying the encounter.

Later, I met with his wife to check out my information. "You are correct," she said. "He was so close to death that I never left his bedside without telling myself that in all likelihood this was my final farewell. But he would never admit it. Even to this day we cannot talk about it. He assumes that it is life as usual, and it is not that for me. I need to believe that I have received a second chance with my husband, and I need to capitalize on every moment I have. If he knew how much of my positive behavior is motivated by having been so close to losing him, he would be horrified. Yet I do have this intense need to talk to him about the horrible crisis I endured. This would be so helpful to me, but he will not allow me."

There is value in a positive optimistic attitude to aid recovery. But perhaps my friend has gone too far. Must one close the door on death to sustain the struggle to live? This incident showed me the enormous denial process that we use to blot out the fact of death and as a result simultaneously diminish the quality of life.

Clyde and Ruth Fretz had no training in how to prepare for death when they clearly heard the trumpet sound. It began with a diagnosis of cancer. Then came the word that it was rapidly advancing and that Ruth should expect to live only six months to one year. From that day on they lived in the shadow of death.

Fortunately Ruth and Clyde had more than 40 years of marriage when they sensitively tuned in on each other. They had never needed many words since they could read each other so well nonverbally. Naturally, conversation about death and dying included only brief exchanges now and then.

Miraculously, Ruth went into quick remission and had three more good years. They accepted this time together as an answer to their prayers for healing. In the fourth year another major collision with death was awaiting them.

During this time Ruth taught Clyde how to do the household chores that he would need to do alone, especially the laundry and preparing meals. She was particularly concerned that he hang the laundry on the line correctly. Although they could not express the exact reason for her teaching him, they both knew.

In the presence of their pastor, Ruth expressed her desire to live a full life and to see her grandchildren grow up since that might not happen. She also expressed readiness to go home whenever the Lord called her.

Clyde and Ruth had a strong faith in God, which they expressed to each other and to other people. Today Clyde cherishes their conversations and finds them helpful in accepting his loss of her.

In reflecting now, Clyde knows that he and Ruth did communicate many things nonverbally. One reason they did not speak more about her impending death was that they both sensed each other's weaknesses. To have brought up the subject directly would have taken an emotional toll, and neither had energy to spare. Now he occasionally regrets that they did not say more. It would feel good to know exactly what Ruth was thinking. Her direct words about death would be helpful in his healing.

They did face one issue directly, however. Several weeks before her death Ruth stated that she preferred to die at home rather than in the hospital, and they were able to arrange for this. As Ruth grew weaker, Clyde stayed at her side as much as he could. During one night he noticed that she was slipping away. For half an hour he held her hand as her breathing became more labored. Then, with one slight tremor, she was gone. Ruth's death was very peaceful—a precious moment shared between two people who had been close to each other.

One legacy that Ruth gave Clyde was an essay she had copied from an unknown source in anticipation of her death. This suggests that, in fact, they had faced death together even if not in specific in-depth conversation.

FIVE MINUTES LATER

It may be in a moment, or after months of waiting, but soon I shall stand before my Lord—perhaps this year.

Then, in an instant all things will appear in new perspective.

Suddenly the things I thought important—tomorrow's tasks, the plans for the dinner at my church, my success or failure in pleasing those around me—these will matter not at all. And the things to which I gave but little thought—the word about Christ to the man next door, the moment (how short it was) of earnest prayer for the Lord's work in far-off lands, the confessing and forsaking of that secret sin—will stand as real and enduring.

Five minutes after I'm in heaven I'll be overwhelmed by the truths I've known but somehow never grasped. I'll realize then that it's what I am in Christ that comes first with God, and that when I am right with him, I do the things which please him.

I'll sense that it was not just how much I gave that mattered, but how I gave—and how much I withheld.

In heaven I'll wish with all my heart that I could reclaim a thousandth part of the time I've let slip through my fingers, that I could call back those countless conversations which could have glorified my Lord, but didn't.

Five minutes after I'm in heaven, I believe I'll wish

with all my heart that I had risen more faithfully to read the Word of God and wait on him in prayer—that I might have known him while still on earth as he wanted me to know him.

A thousand thoughts will press upon me, and though overwhelmed by the grace which admits me to my heavenly home, I'll wonder at my aimless earthly life. I'll wish—if one may wish in heaven—but it will be too late.

Heaven is real and hell is real, and eternity is but a breath away. Soon we shall be in the presence of the Lord we claim to serve.

Why should we live as though salvation were a dream—as though we did not know?

"To him that knoweth to do good, and doeth it not, to him it is sin."

There may yet be a little time. A new year dawns before us. God help us to live now in the light of a real tomorrow.

Just Think
Of stepping on land and finding it heavenly,
Of touching a hand and finding it the Father's,
Of breathing new air and finding it celestial,
Of waking up in glory and finding it home.
—Ruth Fretz

Helping Children Express Grief

On Sunday evening Andrew Fischer had come home after teaching a first-communion class. His wife, Joyce, had put the two boys to bed and remained upstairs. She heard her husband walk across the kitchen floor, and then she heard something fall. When he did not answer her call, she went downstairs and found him in the dark at the foot of the basement stairs. He had fallen down the stairs, head first, and was unconscious. In that split second, Drew Fischer's skull had been fractured, his life blood already spilling onto the hard concrete floor.

Joyce summoned an ambulance, the paramedics did what they could there and rushed Drew to the hospital. Joyce called a neighbor to stay with the boys and waited while doctors worked feverishly to determine the damage and stem the flow of blood. At 3:00 a.m., concerned that the boys might awaken, she returned home.

This is the story of one sensitive mother who guided her children on an exemplary journey through grief. Perhaps it can provide hope for parents of other children who have to handle prematurely a loss that is too great for them to carry alone.

The first thing I remember about the boys was that they slept through the night. I could not think of anything more horrible than having them wake in the middle of all the trauma of ambulances, paramedics, or even waking up when I was at the hospital to discover that I was gone and Dad was gone and there was a neighbor in the house. It was someone they knew but not someone who belonged there in the middle of the night, and I was glad they did not have to hear from the neighbor what had happened.

My first feelings had to do with how glad I was that they had slept and that I did not have to deal with them during those first hours when I didn't know what was happening either. I had no problem leaving them sleep. The neighbor suggested waking them and taking them to her house to sleep, but I couldn't think of anything worse than waking them up and saying, "You have to get up. Your dad's unconscious, and we're taking him to the hospital. I don't know what's happening, but you have to get up and go over to the neighbor's and wait until I come back sometime tomorrow and tell you about it." So I resisted waking them in the middle of the night. I was amazed that they slept through it. There was a lot of commotion—sirens and lights flashing, and the paramedic yelling at Drew to see if he could regain consciousness. We had to dismantle a shelf to get him out of the basement, so there was all that commotion and yet they stayed asleep.

I came back from the hospital about 3:00 a.m., and I waited until about one half hour before the time I always woke them. I told them as calmly as I could what had happened, but I told them the truth about it. I didn't try to say that he was going to be okay. I told them that the doctor didn't know whether he would live—that there was a possibility he would die.

I woke George first. He was eleven. When I told him, his response was to turn over in the bed, beat on his pillow, and to cry and say, "It isn't fair! It isn't fair!" I assured him that I agreed with him completely. It definitely was not fair, but it had definitely happened. Then, when George was calmer, he went with me into Peter's room and we woke Peter and told him. Peter was seven. I don't remember exactly what Peter's response was except that I have the impression that he never answered me. For several days after that when we talked about it Peter would listen, but would not respond verbally. He responded by body language. He would sit in his chair, as far back in the corner as he could get with his arms folded across his chest.

The boys decided that they would like to go school, and they did go. They went to school every day that week while Drew was in the hospital. Their teachers were told and knew what had happened when the children came in.

By the time they arrived home from school that first day, my mother had arrived from South Carolina, so there was some excitement about seeing her unexpectedly, which eased things for them.

Monday was Halloween. Trick-or-treating had always been a big thing at our house. We had spent a lot of time making costumes, and they seemed rather desperate to hang on to what was familiar and so they went trick-or-treating. We had the usual family discussion about how long they could stay out. They wanted to stay out much longer than I was willing to agree.

We finally compromised, but they were not out long before they came back in saying not many homes were ready to receive trick-or-treaters. So Monday night we tried to be as normal as we could under the circumstances.

I told them as carefully and as best I could what was happening to Drew physically and medically and asked them if they would like to visit him in the hospital. They said they would, so I arranged to take George and Peter in on Tuesday night. The nurses recommended that we come at the end of the visiting *hours so a lot of people would not be staring at the boys to see what their reactions would be.*

Before we left home, I explained to them what they would see—that their dad would be in bed as though he were asleep, with a bandage around his head, that he would be very still, that he would not respond to them, and that there would be a lot of tubes and machines. We talked about it.

When we arrived at the hospital, a nurse met (came out to meet) us and carefully described the machines—the heart monitor, the respirator. He was on IVs and receiving oxygen. We walked into the room. George turned very pale and sat down immediately. Peter marched over to his dad, put his hand on his shoulder, and said, "Well, Dad, I thought about bringing you a piece of my trick-or-treat candy, but I was afraid it would get stuck in that tube." And he patted and rubbed his shoulder for a while. After a while George was able to go over to the bedside too. The nurse came back in and asked if they had any questions; George did. She had to explain again exactly what everything was for and what it was doing.

We didn't stay more than 15 minutes and went home again. In the car George said to me, "That wasn't nearly as bad as I thought it was going to be!" And I thought, "Oh, my, if that wasn't as bad as he thought it was going to be, what was he thinking?" How could it have been any worse? I remembered his reaction when he walked in—I thought he was going to faint—yet the reality wasn't as bad as his imagination. What was he imagining? What goes on in the mind of a child at the time of a crisis like this?

As I reflect on this incident, I know I did the right thing. I know George well enough to know that he does not want me to probe into his deep emotional life. So I chose not to ask him to tell me what he was anticipating. He knew he could tell it and I would ac-

cept it. We had developed that kind of an understanding long before this.

Yet I do know that most parents should take an occasion like this to help children put their terror into words. Children usually need help to bear a weight like this. We went back to the hospital after visiting hours again on Thursday night. The visit had been arranged ahead of time, and George walked in and noticed that the heart monitor was not showing the same design that it had shown before. He immediately got very upset and said, "What's wrong?" I didn't know what was wrong, so he got the nurse, and asked, "What's wrong with Dad? What's wrong with my dad's heart? It's not looking like it looked the time we were in before?" The nurse kept saying, "There's nothing wrong with your dad's heart." And George would say, "That doesn't look the way it looked when we were here before." So the nurse took both Peter and George out to the nurses' desk and compared Drew's EKG strip to a strip of someone who was in with a heart attack to assure them that what they were thinking was not true, that his heart was still performing properly.

In retrospect, I believe I may have missed a hidden message here. I permitted the nurse to do all the explaining. Perhaps we all needed to deny the reality of Drew's condition. It was as if she were saying, "Look how good your dad's heart is; he will live." But then that is what we all may have needed to hear at that time. Maybe I could have said to George later, "Now remember, George, it is not Dad's heart that is the problem. It is what happened to his head." After all, two days later his brain ceased functioning altogether.

At that time I tried to stay aware of the boys' emotions, while I was trying to cope with my own tumultuous emotions. While they were losing their father, I was losing my husband.

On Friday afternoon, both the neurosurgeon and the neurologist on the case told me that they could tell me there was absolutely no hope and that it was just a matter of time—but they couldn't tell me how much time. When the electroencephalogram indicated that his brain waves had gone flat, he could be pronounced legally dead.

After I went home on Friday night, I remembered that I had still not told anyone there that Drew had wished to be an organ donor; so I called back to the hospital and gave them that information. I discovered later that they had already discontinued a lot of the medication that was designed to keep body functions normal in case there was some hope of recovery; but when they found this out, they immediately put him back on everything to keep his body as normal as possible.

Early Saturday morning the doctor called to say (tell me) I should come to the hospital right away. When I arrived, he informed me that the transplant team was waiting for me to see Drew for the last time—that the brain wave was flat and it was all over. So I called back home and one of the neighbors brought my mother and George and Peter. I called Drew's family and they also came to the hospital. Of course I had to tell the boys that when they went in that everything would look exactly the same as on Thursday and on Tuesday, but this time Drew was dead. So we all went for the last time.

Later, I learned that when they arrived at their grandparents' home, George called his best friend. When the friend asked, "How's your dad?" George replied, "I can describe how my dad is in just one word: dead!"

The boys and I had a very open relationship, so a lot did not have to be put into words. With their dad they had a continuous verbal relationship. With me it was that we could sensitively experience each other,

although it was nonverbal. Since this was estab-
lished long before, it would not suddenly change
now.

We did talk about Drew. We talked about the fact
that God would take care of him, and we talked
about praying for him. One of the things that I remember Peter did was he would always listen but
would not participate in our conversations. He would
take a piece of paper and he would write out his
prayers. "Dear God, please don't let my daddy die!"

As soon as I recognized that Peter wasn't going to
talk to me, I called Paulette, the school counselor,
and she began seeing him. He talked to her. She said
that he would come in and sit down and start talking. She would only direct or occasionally ask a
question to direct the conversation. So he had a
tremendous need to talk, but not with me. Maybe he
thought it would hurt me to talk about Drew's death.

It was difficult, and it still is, to know how much to
nudge either of them to talk about Drew's death. I
sometimes will bring it up in conversation to give
them the opportunity if they want to. George simply
closes it off and says, "I don't know." Peter either
changes the subject or leaves if he doesn't want to
talk. So I have never really had what I would
consider a good conversation about what happened
with either of them. If I felt that there were things that
I wanted them to know, they would listen to what I
told them, but they have never responded much.
Even my respecting that right was valuable. That's
the reason I've been so grateful that Paulette has had
rapport with Peter and he would talk to her so will-
ingly.

Drew had always requested that he not have a
public viewing. So that was not a decision I made—
that was one of his requests that I followed. We used
a local funeral home so the director knew Drew very
well from having worked with him at funerals. Her

husband had also died, leaving her with three children. They were older when their father died, but she at least had the experience of knowing that there were some special things that needed to be done because there were children. I arranged with her that we would go to the funeral home on Monday evening as a family, privately.

Drew looked quite good. They had managed to hide all of the wounds. Peter noticed immediately that he didn't have his glasses on. I had not sent the glasses to the funeral home when I sent his clothes, but I had the glasses in my purse. He said, "He just doesn't look right without his glasses." I said, "Well, I have them with me. Would you like for him to have them on?" He said, "Yes!" So I gave them to the director and she cleaned them and placed them on Drew's face. Peter seemed more satisfied and went over and patted Drew. The rest of us were sitting down and the whole action was Peter's. He was totally engrossed in what was going on. For the rest of us to have done anything would have disrupted what was happening with Peter.

Peter approached his father's coffin alone and gently, his face masking all expression.

My sister had taken him shopping that day to buy him a new jacket and he was proud of it. He needed a winter jacket. It was exactly what he wanted—the kind with sleeves that zip out—and the zipper on the front had a little tab on it with the logo from the manufacturer.

I knew that the tab was an important symbol for Peter. He valued it, but he needed to give a treasured gift to his dad. He reached down and took the tab off the zipper and he tucked it inside the breast pocket of Drew's suit. It was his last gift, so he gave his best.

Then he asked me if I had paper and pencil. I found a piece of paper and a pencil for him and without saying any more he just wrote "Love you!"

and signed it "Peter." Then without saying a thing to anybody—no words were used at all—he took it to everybody who was sitting there and had them sign their names. He folded it up and tucked it inside Drew's pocket along with the logo from his jacket. He came over and sat down on my lap and was very quiet. After a while, he said he was ready to go home and so we left.

I was a little surprised. I was disappointed that it had not occurred to me, or that someone had not thought to tell me, that Peter and George might have liked to leave something tangible in the casket with Drew. I found out later that this is not an unusual thing for children to do.

I was very calm. I was not crying. I simply watched this child in amazement and wondered what was going on inside of him. He was doing something that I had not thought about—as hard as I was trying to think of everything. His needs seemed to be so different from his brother's.

George was acting like the adults. He simply was sitting there. I have no idea what was going on inside his head. Neither of them ever cried, other than the first time when I woke George and told him. Peter frequently cried about other things for a while, and I know the other things were just an excuse. He probably was crying for his father. For some reason I expected them to cry and that I would have to comfort them, but that never happened.

We had a public memorial service on Thursday night. The bishop helped plan the service, and we chose a joyful, triumphant theme. George assisted with serving communion. He also sang in the children's choir. It had always been a pleasure to assist his dad, and this one last opportunity was very special.

The funeral was private the next morning. The bishop came to the house before we went to the *funeral home and spoke with George and Peter. He told them that his father had died too when he was a little child. He told them what he would do as far as the funeral was concerned. When we went to the cemetery, Peter was disappointed that they did not let him stand and watch them put the dirt in. He wanted to see the whole thing—the casket lowered and the dirt put on. Perhaps I should have stood up for him and insisted that they let him stand there and watch, but it was a little more than I could do. We went back later in the afternoon to see the closed grave. That appeared to satisfy him.*

In the meantime at the house a lot of people were coming and going. I really felt that the children were being left out in some ways because people came to see me and the conversations were of a nature that the children had no part in them. In a way I had to tell the same story over and over again. Of course the children heard this. People came with a sense of not being able to believe what they heard. Was it really true that this was happening? They brought food, flowers, mail, and our regular routine was disrupted. This was helpful to me. Looking back, I think that was not helpful to the children.

When they asked me if they could bring food in the evenings I said yes. I knew that people were hurting and wanting to do something and there was nothing they could do. If it was going to make them feel better to cook for us, that was okay and I'd certainly be happy to eat it. That also meant I didn't have to think about what to cook.

One day Peter was visibly upset and almost screamed, "Everybody in the whole world knows my daddy's dead and the half of them are bringing us food." Then I realized that this bothered him; so I asked that the food be stopped, and we went back to preparing our own food. We were eating much better and more nutritiously when others were preparing food for us. Again it was the disruption of family routine that seemed to bother Peter quite a lot. The lady who was in charge of organizing the meals understood when I explained that this was upsetting him.

It all added up to deciding whose need must take precedence: the people from the church or my sons. They needed to feed us to deal with their grief, but Peter needed them not to do it. So I chose Peter's need above theirs.

I can't imagine what all those two boys went through. I know how difficult it was for me. Yet I had enough life experience to realize that even though I didn't know that day what was going to happen to us, we were going to be all right—that I could manage and that the church was not going to just throw us away. But when they lost their father, they lost their security because he was the dominant person in their lives in the family. We planned our family schedule around Drew's schedule. He was the one who brought home the paycheck and they knew that. We lived in a parsonage because he was the pastor; so even our home depended on him. Then to have all of that taken away—the uncertainty about what was happening to them—I just can't even imagine what they might have been thinking. They were thinking because both of the boys are thinkers.

I don't remember any special conversations, but I was constantly trying to give them information to know that everything was going to be all right. My mother kept saying, "You can always come home and live with me." There was never any time that we were homeless. The church council acted immediately and said, "Don't think about moving. You can stay here at least until school is out, and Drew's salary will be continued for three months." It was not as though we were going to be evicted. It was just that it was a while before I could say to them, "Yes,

we do have enough money. We can buy a house." I
wasn't sure what my resources were. As I knew this, I
kept them informed. I even told them when I knew
they might not understand what I was saying. I tried
to help them see that though things would never be
the same, we were going to be okay.

Even though my mother lived with us at that point,
the boys still had to know where I was every minute.
I had to be there when they left for school; and I had
to be there when they came home, or they had to
know where I was and when I would be home. They
were never alone, but still they had to be sure that I
was okay and that I would be back. It was extremely
important for them to know that I would be there. I
did not have to do something with them directly.
They just needed to know where I was.

Peter still is struggling with this. For him to go to
camp this summer I had to make arrangements to
call every day so he would know that I'm okay. Even
though it's been almost two years since his dad died,
he needs to know that he hasn't lost me while he's
gone.

During the early grief process Peter and I had one
brief conversation about school. He said that sometimes he got so busy in school that he didn't think
about dad. He wondered if that was okay. I assured
him that there were times when I got busy and didn't
think about Drew either, so it was okay not to think
about him all the time.

Some months after Drew died—when it was obvious that we were going to be all right and were in
the process of buying a house—Peter said that every
now and then when he was little he would think
about the possibility that Mom or Dad could die. He
just didn't believe it would ever happen; but now that
it happened, he guessed it was good that it had been
Dad who died. It was almost as though he was saying, "I really didn't know if we could manage without

Dad, but now I know we can. But I still can't imagine it being the other way. I still don't know what would have happened if it had been Mom who died instead of Dad." I know he was thinking about things even when he wasn't talking a lot.

I kept telling them that God would take care of us and that he acted through other people. This was illustrated for us beautifully when a scholarship fund was started by other pastors and church friends. Contributions continue to come in for the trust fund.

Christmas was not as difficult as I had anticipated. There were still a lot of family around and special things going on, so we didn't sit around and feel sorry for ourselves.

When the school counselor was talking with Peter, she occasionally called me to assure me that Peter was grieving but was okay. It was a normal kind of grief and he was working through it pretty well. During one of our conversations, she told me that when he came into her room, he went to the chalkboard and drew the picture of a tombstone—a tall oval shape, rounded at the top, the kind of thing that children think about when they think of tombstones. He had written "SUPERDAD" on it. I filed that bit of information away.

When the time came an appointment was made and the owner was told that the children would be coming along and choosing the marker.

One Saturday morning we went to pick out the stone. I had told them that they could make all the decisions and they weren't to worry about how much it cost. They were just to pick out what they thought was right—what we would be happy with. We must have been there for a good two hours. They examined every one, and they finally came to some decisions. It had to be white—not black, gray, or pink. It had to be smooth all over with no rough edges. They decided how big they wanted it and what shape it was to be. Then we came to deciding what should be put on it.

Peter sat down with a paper and drew a number of different pictures. The owner showed us designs similar to Peter's and we talked about them. Peter said—and George agreed with him—that it should say, "SUPERDAD"; then in smaller letters it should say "Pastor Fischer," when he was born, and when he died. They allowed me to make it "Pastor Andrew Fischer." They understood that his first name should be there too.

Peter chose a design close to his own, and Mr. Ziegler started drawing up copies. Every once in a while he excused himself, and I noticed that he was crying and going into a back room to wipe his eyes. Watching Peter and George do this was more than he could take calmly. He came up with some alternative wordings to Superdad, but nothing would suit. It had to say Superdad. I knew he was having trouble with that wording, so finally I said, "I bet there's not another marker in the whole world that says 'Superdad.'" He said, "No, I don't think there is." I said, "Well, you understand, don't you? This one has to say 'Superdad.'" He said yes.

About four months later the stone was put up. When I was informed about it, I took Peter in the car and we went out. I asked Peter, "Is it okay?" He examined it from top to bottom. He would back up 10 paces and would look at it from one angle. Then he went 20 paces and looked at it from another angle. Finally he declared that it was just what he wanted.

All this time I feared that he might find something wrong with it. I didn't know if there was anything that could be done about it if Peter didn't give it his seal of approval, but he did. I'm sure that people wondered whether the children might be embarrassed by it when they grew older. I said it was not

sacred. If they were embarrassed by it, they could re-
place it. But right now that was what needed to be
put on the stone.

One October day, a year later, I said that I was going to a florist to get crysanthemums to put on Dad's
grave and asked Peter if he would like to go along
and help pick them out. When we got there they also
had pumpkins and he asked me if he could buy a little pumpkin. I said, "It's awfully little, Pete. What are
you going to do with that?" He said, "I want to carve
a jack-o-lantern for Dad's grave."

One morning he got up early and decided he had
to carve the pumpkin before he went to school. We
spread out the newspapers and he got his knife and
did it very carefully. When he finished he said, "See, I
did it just the way Dad taught me to do it!" We took it
out to the cemetery and put it on the gravestone. It
stayed there until it dried up. It shriveled to almost
nothing, and if we had not known it was a pumpkin,
we would not have been able to identify it.

I remembered that the Sunday of Drew's accident
was the day Drew and Peter had sat on the kitchen
floor and carved the Halloween pumpkin. I thought,
There's only one gravestone out there marked
"SUPERDAD," and it's the only grave with a jack-o'-
lantern on it. It was another gift to Drew from Peter.

This spring I asked the counselor to see Peter
again because he was depressed and still angry
about his father's death. They had spent time becoming reacquainted. The second time we went she
came out to get me and told me she felt there was a
breakthrough, but she wanted Peter to tell me. When I
went in Peter told me that he felt that he had left a
light on in the basement that night and that his dad
had been on the way down the stairs to turn the light
off and fell. Poor child! He thought he had caused his
daddy's death!

I was absolutely sure that the light was off. I

*quickly reassured him that I had checked it and that
the light was off.*

I know that children often assume that they are
responsible when a parent dies. It never occurred to
me that my son would create an explanation like he
did. He blamed himself for the death.

This helps to explain why he preferred not to talk
about it for so long afterward. He probably had already decided he was to blame and he was not
ready to reveal this secret. Now that this issue was
cleared up he is much more relaxed. What an awful
burden for a young heart to bear. I am so happy that
the right person was ready to listen and deal with it
when he was ready to share his feelings.

Last fall one of our friends was dying with a brain
tumor. Peter was sick and stayed home from school
the day the man's wife and two of her children came
over, so Peter and her sons played together. She was
deeply concerned about how to prepare the boys for
the time when it really happened. She had a real
dread about going to the cemetery, but she went
along with us to see Drew's marker. The two boys,
Peter, and I went over. She began to feel that it was
really rather nice and was not that horrible a place.
It was a mild fall day and we picked pinecones, and
looked around at all the people we had known who
were buried there. We were talking about various
ways to help children deal with the whole thing.
Peter was listening and really concentrating. So I
asked Peter, "Do you have any suggestions? What
can Steven's mommy do to help Steven and Mi-
chael?" And he said, "Well, you know how I kept
something of Dad's. She can be sure to save some of
his things for her children."

It's been two years now since Drew died, and the
boys have grown happier and more secure. I have
tried to reinforce the idea that we can use what has
happened to us to help other people. I think the boys

understand this. Helping people is certainly not a new idea to them. Their father modeled it with his life.

Occasionally I have the opportunity to say, "I can't do it all by myself. We must allow others to help us fill in the gaps." They accept that, but I'm sure they don't realize how people have helped fill in those gaps. I've learned to accept that kind of help and even to ask for it on their behalf. Alone, I could never have given them the kind of help they've received from teachers, guidance counselors, parents of their friends. and others. One day I will help them understand that God has cared for them through these people.

One of the things that seems to have helped George a lot was the fact that his dad's corneas and kidneys were donated for transplants. I remember Peter wanting to take the letter of acknowledgment from the transplant director to show to the principal at school. The boys have taken a great deal of comfort in knowing that two people could see and two people were alive because of their dad—a deep and meaningful symbol that something good can come from a tragedy.

It's hard to accept that I can't just put a bandaid on the wound. I watch for signs that it's time for Peter to talk to the guidance counselor. I've accepted that he isn't going to talk to me about his loss.

George uses his great ability to think and deals with his grief internally. I am concerned that it may all come flooding out at an inconvenient or inappropriate time for him."

If nothing else, this story should serve to remind us that, when it comes to grief, children often speak a different language. Among children, there is a need for action. Sincere, satisfying gestures of reassurance. Gestures that include things that seem irrelevant or immaterial to adults. Things like eyeglasses and jacket logos, like jack-o'-lanterns and tombstones.

Words are not as important to children. Having only partially developed their language skills, actions *do* speak louder than words for them.

Perhaps we also ought to remember that we are all children at heart, and that we all have the need to "do" symbolic acts as well. The giving of the dead one's clothing to a worthy charity or recipient helps us return again to life, satisfied that we have carried out their wishes or extended their influence. The need for action does not disappear as we grow older. It only gets covered up.

Unhealthy Dying and Unhealthy Grieving

Karen and Kirk were both seminary graduates. Kirk was ordained to the pastoral ministry. Because of questions their church had about women in ministry, Karen was never ordained. This did not deter her from very active participation in ministry, including preaching. When I first met this couple they were in their early thirties and childless. The fact that Karen was suffering from cancer brought them to my office.

Karen appeared to have a more dynamic personality. She glowed with excitement. Kirk had some difficulty talking. It was apparent that he gained many ideas and much inspiration from her.

In college Karen had majored in music and had taken a special course in church organ music. In addition to being a pastor's wife, she directed the music program of the church, conducted the choir, and provided special music.

After listening to the story of their seven years of marriage, I had a deep sense of the complementation of their personalities and got the impression that there was little conflict. Although they were quite different, this enhanced their marriage and ministry rather than impaired it.

Karen and Kirk had heard about my work with the terminally ill and called for an appointment. I found it difficult to discover the real reason they sought help. The central theme of their conversations about the illness was that together they were going to conquer it. I knew that I had no role in that task. I was willing to help them accept death, but that was not what they wanted.

When I inquired about the treatment history, they described weeks of chemotherapy with all the side effects, including blisters in her mouth and repeated loss of hair. There were brief periods of remission, but none of sustained duration. Yet, beyond all medical evidence, together they were going to rise above all this and survive. They believed that it was God's will that Karen should live. They had memorized all the verses of Scripture that support miraculous healing.

One time when I heard them say that God's response would be directly related to their diligence in prayer, I became concerned. Since that was an awesome burden to put upon themselves, I challenged this ever so gently. Karen emphatically stated their belief and then enumerated instances of Kirk's doubting, or failing to persevere in prayer. At each of these times there had been a relapse. After this I began to feel my own pain. What would happen to Kirk if their demand to live was not granted?

Several weeks earlier Karen had asked Kirk if she might bring the morning message at church. Kirk had always agreed, so why not now? He assumed that she would take the occasion to tell the congregation about their struggle with the illness and to talk about her hope for life thereafter. She said nothing about that. Instead she did a fantastic presentaion about the power of Christ to direct lives, with the power to heal all ills. The congregation was mesmerized by her performance and many told her that they would pick up the challenge to pray fervently for her so that she might live.

As Kirk and Karen told more of their story, I received

the distinct impression that death was simply re-
moved from her schedule, and with Kirk's help she
was going to conquer it. She appeared to be on a white
horse charging ahead proclaiming victory over death.
The ultimate outcome would be that jointly they would
have a powerful ministry in the church. This required
greater faith, and they would show the way.

Even as death was coming closer and closer, Karen's
message became clearer and clearer. She wrote exten-
sive letters to family, friends, and congregation members. Those who received the letters could not believe
that she had written them, and least of all that she was
dying.

I tried to introduce some reality into her life, but to
no avail. She even accused me of lacking faith and that
I would cause Kirk to doubt more. Then, by implica-
tion, she would die and it would be our fault. There appeared to be no resolution possible. I was never able to
determine clearly why they had sought help. They
ended their sessions on this confused note.

Within a few months I read Karen's obituary in the
newspaper. Several months passed before Kirk called
for help at the strong urging of his bishop.

From Kirk I learned that Karen had not changed her
position at any time. Even on the very last day when
she was fading in and out of consciousness, she used
whatever strength she could muster to rally him on
with the same denial. Finally, when Karen faded into
death, Kirk became helpless. The church granted him
a three-month leave of absence; and the bishop had
the leave conditioned upon his seeking help.

Karen's memorial service had been one of grand
celebration. Kirk delivered a eulogy. He collected many
of her letters written during the weeks preceding her
death and read them. The congregation understood

these victory passages to mean that Karen was preparing for the victory that she had now inherited in heaven. The truth, however, was that eternal victory had nothing to do with it. For Karen, victory meant cure. Many stood up during the service and witnessed about Karen's courage and inspiration. It had been uplifting for them to watch her reach the greatest height of victorious living when she was closest to death. This gave them the inspiration to live and die courageously as they assumed she had done.

Now Kirk was becoming aware that people had really not heard her message. They heard what they had wanted to hear. Her great rejoicing was really one grand denial-of-death ceremony. Kirk had participated in it because he could do nothing else. He could not even permit himself to doubt her stance in the weeks following her death. This, in itself, was betraying her program, so he could not really grieve.

I observed that Karen had completely controlled the dying process due to her own terror. At no time could she take into account that Kirk also had needs, that after she was gone he would be left holding an empty bag. I told him that was causing his pain now.

Then Kirk told me about his inability to cope. He was remaining in bed until noon almost every day. Preparing meals was an impossible task, so he ate whatever he could take from the refrigerator without preparing it. He spent hour after hour lying on the sofa watching television.

All of this was out of character for Kirk. He and Karen always made fun of "the stupid tube" and refused to watch much television. Now he was attached to it. He had not yet been able to return to a church service, least of all to take charge.

For the next several months we reviewed the entire

dying process many times. This time I could help him understand how totally this had been controlled by Karen to meet her need. It had completely ignored his need. As a result, he was paying the penalty now.

After a while Kirk attempted to circulate in public places. He went to restaurants to find someone with whom to talk. He even bought meals for persons who permitted him to talk. Inevitably, he spent the time talking about Karen. After he returned home, he realized that he knew nothing about the person with whom he had conversed. The worst sensation came when he talked to women and later realized that he had expected them to respond like Karen. When they responded differently, he became annoyed. He also began to question whether he might ever begin again, because he would always compare other women to Karen. Since no one would be exactly like Karen, no one would be good enough.

Six months later, he ended counseling. He had returned to the pulpit, but he could not bear the thought of a future courtship.

Everything about Karen and Kirk was programmed to live and nothing was programmed to die. But death came knocking on their door anyway. They responded by refusing to answer the knock. They pretended not to hear. They assumed that they could turn away the unwelcome guest. The harder they tried, the more they punished themselves.

Karen led the way in this denial process; but she had led the way in living also. She was the vivacious outgoing one. Kirk was withholding, reluctant, and hesitant. Her grand design for living included more adventure than he needed, more impact on people than he made, more work in the kingdom of God than he envisioned.

Karen joined Kirk in seminary education, even though she knew the church was not ready to accept her. In spite of these odds, and without official sanction, she was involved in all forms of ministry. She was never deterred. During my brief encounter with her, I got the distinct impression that she had a dynamic personality and could make things happen. She did not retreat in fear in the face of obstacles; she merely gathered momentum until she overcame the obstacles.

Kirk needed and thrived on Karen's enthusiasm and example. When he did not know the way or have the courage to move, he simply turned to Karen and received direction and the drive to succeed. If he could not, or would not, accomplish a task, she would do it.

This style was great for living, but it was a huge handicap for dying. It is easy to believe and feel that Karen should not be the person to be beckoned by death. It is understandable that her leaving would be an enormous loss to Kirk and to the church.

It is not that Karen was so afraid to die. She did not fear pain, the dying process, nor life after death. It was simply that death did not fit her schedule, nor her schedule for Kirk.

It is as if an Olympic athlete had spent all her life preparing for the final event, and then just before the race, she was disqualified. Not to arrive at the final destination is extremely difficult to accept when you have spent years striving in that direction.

Karen used everything in her power to deny the knock on her door. She even adjusted her spiritual life to fill this need. She claimed the scriptural promises and commanded all to obey so she might live. She told everyone who knew her that they had only to invoke the power of God and she would live. Karen also believed that the reverse was true; if her health failed, then all had failed. She declared God was willing and ready to heal if the request was sufficiently diligent and persistent. However, death was not to be deterred. At the appointed time death visited.

Then Kirk paid a penalty for their lack of preparation. He had not only lost a special companion, he had also lost the ability to live afterward. He could not make the emotional journey back that he needed to make. Every time he tried, he faced the enormous unresolved conflict that Karen had left behind. As soon as he tried to resolve the conflict, he viewed the scene of her proclaiming life, not death, from the pulpit. He saw the congregation responding wholeheartedly to her zeal. He could not face the fact that Karen was proclaiming one message while the congregation heard another.

For Karen victory over death meant to remain alive bodily; for the congregation victory meant that the resurrected life was awaiting her. To make peace with her death meant that Kirk had to admit that his beloved Karen was wrong in her understanding of life-and-death, God, faith, obedience, and prayer. Next, he had to arrive at a new understanding for himself. His dependence on Karen and the toll from his loss and grief resulted in his inability to move; he numbly remained on the sofa staring at "the stupid tube."

What could this couple have done to change the drama?

First, they should have acknowledged that when death came knocking, they needed to listen. They should have taken a closer look at the Scriptures. Yes, it is God's will that humankind should live, but that will has been thwarted by the fall. Death is inevitable for everyone. Miracles do happen, but God will not erase our finite nature. Karen also should have recognized the truly greatest miracle of all time—that eternal life comes only after death. If Karen had yielded, she might have taught Kirk how to yield to grief and to his loss. In yielding to his loss he would have found courage to turn again to life.

Death is sad enough, but when it leaves survivors too crippled to grieve it is even more destructive. If survivors cannot take the emotional journey back, they cannot live again. The past must be settled before grieving ones can accept an invitation to live.

A Battered Heart Finds Courage

When I awoke I already knew that I could not face life. I pulled the covers over my head and curled up. Even thinking was painful, so I lay there as near to a zombie as possible.

After I finally got up I had this gnawing sensation that I couldn't live without J.J. I kept pacing the floor. At times I could get involved in doing what had to be done, but soon I was walking aimlessly again. There was a strange dread in my stomach. As noon approached, it got worse. Then I discovered what really was wrong. Repeatedly, I found myself walking over to the front window, opening the curtains, and looking out. Suddenly I realized that I was expecting him to come home for lunch. He worked at a hardware store across the street. He was supposed to be here for lunch. No matter how often I look, it doesn't help, he simply doesn't come.

Every day I have to push myself to get through the day, but today the weight is more than I can push. I simply am not strong enough today.

It is not that I am so weak. It is only that death has hit me so often and so hard that I had all my energy knocked out.

J.J.'s death is only the latest of six deaths. This son's car struck the concrete abutment of a utility pole late one night when he was returning home. At just 20 years of age, he was killed instantly.

When I was 12 years of age my 22-two-year-old brother died in a car accident. My father died of cancer 16 years ago. Then about 12 years ago my only nephew, Jeff, died of leukemia. My only living brother, Jeff's father, vanished shortly after that. Three and one half years ago our 11-year-old son, John John, was mowed down in front of our house by a car. Then, finally, it was J.J. This means every male on my side of the family is dead.

For three and a half years I struggled tenaciously to make the life and death of my other son, John John, be meaningful, but this death did me in. I have run out of steam.

You see John John was our youngest child and he was born with Down's Syndrome. For the 11 years he lived, he and I, with the rest of the family, proved that a retarded child could succeed.

John John was a great inspiration to a lot of people. Even the local newspaper wrote three annual feature stories on him. The same reporter came to the funeral and again wrote a major article on him. When Eunice Kennedy Shriver came to town a picture was taken with John John and her and this, too, was published. It was a big picture. It showed her bending over John John. There was something about him that attracted people. They stood outside for hours to get into the church at his funeral. All of this publicity made his death easier to bear, since everyone knew what I had lost.

Throughout John John's life I took leadership in helping create new services for the retarded. I championed every cause I could because I knew it was up to parents to fight for the handicapped. They can't do it themselves.

I had to build my life around similar people. Families with Down's Syndrome children have to unite to build services and to support each other. Suddenly John John was gone, but I continued to be involved. I had learned so much that I had a lot to give to this cause. This helped me. This kept John John's life meaningful as I carried out what he

helped me begin. I would never have been involved if
it hadn't been for John John.

But now children with Down's syndrome bother
me. They keep reminding me of John John. They look
so similar that I can't help it. This happens even
though I believe each handicapped child is very different—very special and unique in his own way. By
now my middle daughter is married and expecting a
child. Can you imagine what is going through my
head? If she gives birth to a boy, he, too, is doomed to
die young. Males don't make it in my family! Even if
he is all right, I still have to constantly dread the
possibility that at any time, when I least expect it, the
telephone may ring again to bring the dreadful news
once more. For my welfare it had better be a girl.
Then I could give my system a break and relax. Isn't
it terrible to think this way?   I even avoid my
daughter now. I should tell her why I'm avoiding her.
She needs me to be a mother to her. I have not even
gone with her to the doctor to hear the heart beat. I
cannot bring up the subject of J.J. in the house. My
husband and my three daughters are hurting as
much as I am. They, too, are struggling to survive.
They have their own way to do it. So how can I expect
them to help me? What makes this worse is that they
know that I am ready to come apart at all times. How
can anyone bring up the subject even if they need to?
They would have to devote all their energies to putting me together. They have barely enough to cope on
their own, so I must go elsewhere for help.

The girls have gone back to see the cement pillar
and the wrecked car. I cannot do it. I cannot drive on
that road. For three months I have totally avoided
even going near that part of town.

You see, it's that concrete reinforcement of the
utility pole that bothers me so much. It was put there
because the pole was repeatedly knocked down; so
the utility company decided to protect their pole at

all cost. Didn't they realize that if the pole was hit continually that it was placed at a dangerous location? When they chose to protect it with concrete didn't they realize that they were trading their pole for someone's life? What they did was erect a sure killer.

Often I wake up at night. Then I start crying in bed. I am afraid I might wake my husband and he has to work the next day. Then I have to get up, so I go downstairs. I drink one cup of coffee after another. I may take one drink. Then I smoke continuously.

We have a houseful of grief and no relief. I even keep wondering if the house should be abandoned— closed up and left alone. Maybe it needs a break from all the sadness and anger.

I am so angry at my husband. He behaves as if nothing happened. He finds fifty million things to do so that there is no time to think. He has three jobs. If that does not keep him busy, he finds things to do around the house. Just work, work, and never stop to talk about it. It even feels good to tell myself that I am ready to walk out on the marriage—just simply call it quits.

I forget that my husband was only 12 when he lost his father. As a result he had to be the man of the house. He had his childhood taken away. He could not break down and cry like I could when my brother died. My husband was the youngest of nine children and was born ten years after the next older one. So he just had to go to work to support his mother. He learned that after a death you work. I know I should understand that he is doing the same thing now— work, work, work. It is no wonder he doesn't know how else to deal with death.

Then the school had an awards banquet where they recognized J.J. I cried and cried. My husband was so embarrassed by me that he told me to stop it. I asked him, "Why don't you cry once in a while?"

He responded, "I can't." That is probably why we are so unable to help each other through this difficult time.

My mother is marvelous. The greater the tragedy that befalls her, the more spiritual she becomes. Now, at 72 years of age, she is not discouraged. She still loves and trusts God. Her faith helped her transcend the loss of her mate, two of her three children, and three of her eight grandchildren. And here I am! I can't even go to church. My cousin who is a nun says that's okay for now.

She has told me that I should talk to God at home—if I can't talk, then scream, or yell at him. He knows what I have gone through. So I do talk to God. I do yell at him—that I hate what he has done.

This coming Sunday I'm scheduled to be a lector, but I told my husband that I'm not ready yet to stand up in front of the whole church to read the lesson. I remember too well what happened after John John's death. I did go to church and cried throughout the whole service. I just don't want people to see me cry again.

It already bothers me so much that people expect me to go on as if nothing happened to my life. "Get over it," is what they seem to be saying. "We have had our difficulties, and we all have to go on. Every life has its trials and tribulations. What makes yours so different?"

"Mine is different," I'd like to scream at them, "because I did pull myself together after the death of my first son, but now I can't." Besides, don't they know that saying those things does not help? It only makes it more difficult for me.

Everyone wants me to get over it. The more they say that, the worse I feel and the less I am able to get over it. What hurts the most is that I see people avoiding me. When I walk down the street, I can see people changing directions because they don't want to meet *me. It's as if I have a strange disease.*

But then, I am no better. There are times when I avoid people too. I also get out of their way, or I hide in the store. I don't want to be reminded, so I have to protect myself.

What really feels bad is to have persons silently stare at me. I feel like Exhibit A in a grief manual. They seem to be checking me out to see if I've gotten over it yet, enough to be approached. That is so cruel. Why don't they just take a chance and approach me?

Grief had a stranglehold on Mary Ann. Hemmed in by her own fears and self-imposed isolation, her life was being choked, constricted into a very small space.

But in the midst of her excruciating pain, this battered heart lifted the phone and called for professional help. In that small, seemingly insignificant moment, her healing began.

As we talked in my office, on park benches, and at other sites, Mary Ann shared her story through heart-wrenching tears as well as releasing laughter. She was tentatively reaching out, watching to see if I could understand the depths of her pain.

We talked of her husband, her children, of the son John John who had also met a violent death, and all the tragic circumstances that you know about now. Together we entered many previously forbidden zones in our conversations. Limping from the battering of her heart, she leaned heavily upon me for courage to talk when she didn't want to. I did my best to listen carefully to this broken heart. It was during this time that a minor miracle occurred—a miracle that marked Mary Ann's healing, and helped her turn again to life.

I had told Mary Ann that I was writing a book and wanted to include her story. I needed to give her a rough draft of this chapter, and it seemed better to take it to her than to mail it. We met at a designated spot near Nazareth, Pennsylvania. This should have been a simple transaction, except that I asked permission to see the infamous concrete pillar and asked directions. Mary Ann said she had no problem with that. She gave us directions, but it caused her to dissolve into tears again. She would not go with us, but drove ahead of us as far as her home.

As if someone were playing a morbid trick on us, an unusually long funeral procession approached us and slowly passed by. My wife and I shared our astonishment at this untimely cortege, but we were more concerned about what was happening to Mary Ann, who was just ahead of us and alone.

We continued on our way to the site and lost Mary Ann in the traffic. At the opposite end of town we easily found the sharp bend in the road and the concrete pillar.

I walked to the post alone. My impression was that this thing was built to withstand any impact. The post was located about eight inches from the roadway, with only an ordinary curb protecting it. You could not have designed a more efficient taker of lives.

I watched the steady flow of traffic coming directly toward this post, before making the sharp bend in the road. The speed limit was 35 miles an hour. Even during the noon hour on a dry, clear day, several tires squealed as they rounded the corner.

I looked at the many scratches and holes in the concrete. Obviously it had suffered many collisions, great and small. There was a large ominous smear of green paint imbedded in an area about three feet high and around half the circumference of the post.

As I looked up, I saw Mary Ann pulling up across the street. This was too much to believe! She had avoided this area for three months. Then she had given me directions to the scene of the accident. But now couldn't handle it.

Mary Ann parked her car quickly and came directly to the dreaded site. Tears rolled down her face, but that did not slow her pace. She reached for me instinctively and we embraced.

This had not been a part of her plans. She had no intentions of coming here. She had followed us. She simply switched off her brain, no longer thinking about her fears, or even about the fact that she was due at work in minutes. It all did not matter. She had entered the most menacing forbidden zone!

Three days later I called Mary Ann to see if she was ready to return the early draft of the manuscript. I wanted to meet her and review the manuscript with her. We met at a public picnic bench and reviewed all the written material as well as the events around the post.

This time Mary Ann spent more time laughing than crying. One reason for the shift was that she was so overwhelmed at the unreal things that were happening. The timing of events was so exact that it could only be accepted as divine leading. She was able to say that she was nearing the point where God could be invited back into her life again.

The ancient Chinese had a forbidden city—a place where no foreigner was permitted, a zone where no Caucasian could set foot. Among my clients, I have observed a similar phenomenon.

Some have forbidden zones—places that they guard, places in their psyche so tender that they will permit no entry. Often they will not even allow themselves to enter this territory.

Sometimes, when I listen with enough love, we enter

those forbidden zones together. Cautiously, tenderly, in our conversations and in their journals, we face what they are afraid to face alone, and then the healing can begin.

The loving therapist or caring friend can give a cup of borrowed courage, courage to tread upon the forbidden ground, and only then can the healing begin.

A Model for Healthy Grieving

For many years I have affirmed that grief counseling is one of the easier types of helping. The problem is never hidden. It is right out in the open and may be discovered by asking. The emotions are also just beneath the surface, so no probing is required. An invitation to share feelings is all that is needed.

After even the most intense sessions with grieving clients, I have concluded that only a small segment of my clinical skill was needed to achieve dramatic results. I believe that everyone can participate in this type of helping in an effective way.

The following model grew out of my interactions with grieving persons. I wish to share this so that the most reluctant helper may find simple guidance and direction in reaching out to those who suffer loss.

The words "Tell me all about it" have become a key to helping others grieve appropriately. This is in direct contrast to the usual comments, "Oh, don't feel so bad," or "You'll get over it." Even worse is, "Don't think about it. Think of all the beauty of life still left for you." Or some kindly soul may remark, "It's God's will, so leave it to him."

The error in this kind of advice is that it is impossible to follow. Feelings cannot be that simply manipulated or programmed by one's mind. If one feels bad, especially over the loss of a loved one, a change of mind or busying oneself does not deal with the hurts. Emotions have to be accepted and handled with tenderness. Deeply hurt feelings heal slowly.

The most harmful element in this kindly advice is that it carries a double messsage. Usually hidden behind the words is an attempt to stop the grieving person from unloading all the intense emotions that lie behind the grief. These emotions have to do with one's own meaning of life and the fact that one's earthly life will end—and perhaps unexpectedly or at least sooner than we desire. Most persons have never faced these questions, not even when they were emotionally able. Now, in the midst of a crisis, they are even less capable of wrestling with such difficult concerns. We have a whole series of euphemisms on file to hand to the grieving, with the unaware but explicit purpose of telling them that we do not want to be forced into dealing with the issues of death. Yet, to help those who are grieving, one must be ready to listen to them and deal with death.

To say, "Tell me all about it," implies that you are ready to listen to whatever the other wants to say and to hear its meaning for both lives. That is no easy task. It is easier to say, "Tomorrow will be better."

Tomorrow will not be better for the grieving ones as long as they meet persons who continue to say this. It will only be better if they can be heard. Otherwise, the grief will have to be buried, and tomorrow it will emerge in one of the many usual symptoms: anger, insomnia, helplessness, guilt, purposelessness, and despair. Grieving persons might get in touch with these feelings if there were someone to reflect them against.

Tomorrow can be better for those who are grieving if we first go with them on an emotional journey backwards. It is yesterday that they need to deal with, not tomorrow. If they can lay yesterday to rest, then they will become available to live tomorrow. If grieving persons can be helped to make peace with the past, then they will be ready to struggle with the future.

As you say, "Tell me all about it," and envision your-self holding out cupped hands, you symbolize to the overwhelmed person that the burden may be placed into your hands and that you are offering to hold it for a time. Slowly the grieving person can begin to take the burden back little by little as he or she is able. The strange phenomenon that occurs is that the biblical admonition to bear one another's burdens (Galatians 6:2) is in fact accomplished. Fully sharing feelings with a genuinely caring person makes the burden only half as heavy because it is now borne by two persons. Mystical or otherwise, seeing persons exclaim their gratitude and express their hope for the future proves that burdens are lighter when shared. Emotional burdens may be shared more easily than financial or material burdens.

This is what grief therapy or grief work is all about: taking the hand of the one overwhelmed with sorrow and walking with that person through the past rela-tionship and returning to the present at the end of your time with them. This has to be repeated until he or she can make the journey without your hand. Then the person is ready to walk into the future with *hope* instead of *despair.*

The grieving person is caught in the present. If one has been unable to let go of the past, one cannot grasp the future. Review the simple facts of the relationship that once existed. Two individuals met at a certain point in time and formed an intimate union. The rela-tionship had both beautiful and stressful moments. Help the individual acknowledge that all relationships have assets and liabilities. When one sees this fact clearly, the door is opened for the grieving person to tell the real story without excessively idealizing the positive and denying the negative. It is helpful to recognize the relationship includes two very significant moments. One is the time when a person realizes the nearness of death. The second is the exact moment of death.

After the death, the experience of the survivor is very rocky at first, especially the funeral arrangements or whatever post-death ritual there may be. It may level off for a period, primarily due to denial or shock. Then when the true impact of life alone hits the person, a new inner turmoil erupts. Some persoons cry out for help and are able to seek it.

In grief counseling it is helpful to go over the simple chronological facts of the past and record them on a chart. As the person tells the date of the marriage, record it. You may wish to include comments that are especially applicable to this grieving individual. For example, the chart becomes more personal if "nightmare due to cancer" is written down as part of the "pre-death process." An arrow that points to the death may extend off the chart and include the comment, "Now with God."

Draw a simple time line marking off the past, the present, and the future. Begin with the present. Ask, "Where are you now?" For most persons in this stage of grief, life does not seem to be worth living. The past is too painful. The future has no meaning. Therefore they forget the present.

This feeling of despair, which is most commonly defined as depression, results because grieving persons attempt to stop time from passing. They do not want the distance between the time when the loved one was with them and the present to increase. The reason for halting time probably is an unconscious attempt to get back to scenes of the past and finish emotional tasks that have not been completed. Simultaneously, the grieving ones are unable to go back because of fear of such intense emotions. Since time cannot be stopped, depression is the only psychological method available. A primary task of grieving is to return emotionally to the past so that one can meet the future with hope rather than despair.

After a brief hearing on the present, you may ask, "How has life been since the funeral?" On this first journey the comments may be simple and emotionally shallow.

Then, ask about the funeral. Ask who came and what relationship they had to the family. A real crescendo of emotions may erupt as the grieving one envisions standing beside the coffin. Then on to the final farewell and the graveside scene.

An even more intense moment is the death scene. This too must be relived. Some people are not able to stop at this on the first journey. They quickly pass over it and continue to talk about their lives together. Take note of this and go with them where they need to go.

The atmosphere may lift as you venture into the past relationship in detail. At first all the good is sorted out, but listen for the other side. It may only be alluded to briefly. This then becomes a cue to pick up the negative.

When you sense that the person's capacity has been reached for this occasion, begin the return journey, picking up a few more new items until you are back to the present. If you are asked, 'What shall I do this week?" A good response is, "Be careful with yourself. You have many hurt feelings. Try not to hurt them more. You may share these with me later. Call me if it gets too painful, and let's talk again."

This entire process can be viewed as the swinging of

a pendulum. Emotionally, the grieving one needs to swing from the present into the past, then through the present to the future again. During healthy grieving, the pendulum swings smoothly. For some people, the pendulum has stopped and they cannot move in either direction. The task in facilitating grief is to begin the swing again.

At first the swings will be short, both toward the past and toward the future. Then the swings become longer, until a full, even swing is achieved. The clock of time is ticking again. Life is lived naturally, taking into account where one has been in life and where one is going, and living both to the full in the present. With each venture into the past, the experience becomes less painful and more consoling. After each return, living in the present becomes more meaningful and the future more hopeful.

Grief becomes healthy when a few goals are achieved. One of these is a need to return to the past, even to the point prior to having met the departed loved one. This puts the relationship into the perspective of the whole. To be aware that there once was a time, even as there now is, when life was lived without the other seems a wholesome approach.

To freely entertain "flashbacks" is essential. The sight of a familiar scene, an item of clothing, the chair where he once sat, or even the recall of her favorite joke will bring an instant replay of the past. One goal should be to permit this to happen periodically or even to cause it to occur deliberately. When it does, pursue the feeling, the scenery, the episode, and play with it as long as you need to. Then peacefully fold it away until it happens again.

The discovery of this grieving model has proved helpful. The journey back will encourage acceptance of many losses, including the loss of youth. It also helps one to yield to finiteness.

I used this model with every person or couple whose stories appear in this book. In some cases I already knew many of the facts about the dying process, but that did not hinder me from asking them to share them. They needed to tell the story for their own healing, so I needed to listen. Then, as they told their stories, I could see stress turn to peace. Bottled-up emotions were vented and thereby dissipated. Festering wounds began to heal. The effectiveness of listening was increased because I considered their stories important enough to share in writing this book. After I returned chapters to them for corrections, I was amazed at how much time and energy they put into enlarging and refocusing the contents. They realized that I was not the only one who would share their loss—a much wider audience would listen.

Then, repeatedly, persons expressed the real anticipation that their written stories would open the way for their friends and relatives to understand. There would be new possibilities for conversations about their losses. It would be easy to call attention to the book and ask others to read "our chapter." The most difficult hurdle would be crossed; the ice would be broken. Following that, it would be appropriate to talk, since someone thought it important enough to write about.

Several people could not wait for the book. They requested copies of their stories immediately. They passed them around to their immediate and extended families. One person asked everyone who visited her house to read her story soon after she received her copy. There was a clear message in her behavior that said, "Read it! Then you will understand what has happened to me. I never thought anyone cared to know. Now you will see that someone understood and considered it worthy to share with others. I hope it's that important to you too."

Maybe Shakespeare already knew everything about this model for grieving when he said: "Give sorrow words: the grief that does not speak whispers the o'er-fraught heart and bids it break."

Let God Do the Mending

The inside of the funeral home reminded me of a cavern—dark, cold, and clammy. Small clusters of people were quietly mumbling or silently staring into space. The recorded music in the background had an eeriness all its own.

In a moment the funeral director descended upon me. His mechanical politeness was almost more than I could stand. I was tempted to tell him to leave me alone until I could get my bearings.

I was looking for the funeral of Becky, a tragic young friend and former client who had killed herself.

I found Bob, Becky's husband, sobbing. He repeatedly thanked me for coming. Then he took me through a heavily draped doorway into a small chapel where Becky's body was in an open casket. "That's not Becky," he said. "It's only what's left."

Becky's face was bloated and bluish, a sharp contrast to her former lean and pale appearance. Bob informed me that in cases of carbon monoxide poisoning the capillary system collapses, making embalming almost impossible. The fluid does not really penetrate the outer surface, which means that much of the blue blood remains to discolor the skin.

The pastor arrived a few minutes before it was time for the service to begin. He looked and acted overwhelmed. He repeatedly apologized that he did not know Becky and Bob and said that he would have only a few words to say.

When I told him that I had prepared a eulogy that I

wished to present, he placed his hand on his forehead and breathed, "Thank God."

The coffin was closed, the drapes of the secluded sanctuary were opened, and the people moved into the few rows of chairs. The pastor and I were directed to designated seats up front. Since I faced the group of about two dozen people, I tried to read their moods. The family was sullen and stone-faced. The few former classmates and friends behind them were expressionless. All were too stunned to cry.

The pastor took his place at the lectern and quickly went through an abbreviated ritual. It was an extremely awkward time for him. He lost his place several times and shuffled his pages desperately. The eerie atmosphere became more dense.

I kept telling myself that this horrible mood must be broken; it could not be left this way. Emotions were so intense that you could almost taste them; yet there was not a tear in the room.

I slowly took my place at the lectern. Silently I opened my book and then looked over the audience. What grim and hopeless faces! I turned toward the casket and with deep feeling said, "Becky," as if addressing her. I could not go on as her father broke into loud tears. A number of tissues rustled, and I began again.

"Becky, you were a very elusive and fragile girl—like the delicacy of expensive china. We knew how fragile you were and we tried to hold you carefully. But one slip of our fingers and you fell and broke into tiny fragments.

You were not made for this world, Becky. It was too cruel and clumsy for your sensitivity. That faraway, silent look often told us that you were seeing another world where you would so much rather be, Your mother was there, and you wanted to be with her. She died at a time when you needed her most—just when you thought you could have her all to yourself. She left far too suddenly, and you never had a chance to say good-bye. Oh, yes, you said, "So long, Mom. See you at the end of the semester." But you didn't mean that to be forever.

Becky, we understand how terribly painful her leaving was for you. When you first mentioned her death, you sobbed and cried like a little child, and then you begged us never to talk about it again. We kept our word. It hurt us even more to know how lonely your grief must have been—that you couldn't even share it. It simply hurt too much.

It gives us comfort to hope that your wish has, at last, been granted. You are now with your mother, and we hope you have her undivided attention forever and ever.

I have confidence that God grants some people the right to choose not to live. I believe he understood that your agony in this life was greater than you could bear and that he will be merciful to you. The misery of life had been so great for you that you saw no other solution. Death to you was the solution to your life, and you did not mean to create the problem that your going has made for us.

Becky, your husband, Bob, loved you. He told you over and over. Even in the final office visit when you screamed at him, struck him, and demanded that he move out of your house and leave you alone, he answered, "I can't, Becky, because I love you." He came back to you over and over again because he loved you, Becky.

He loved you far more than most men love their wives, but we also know that for you it was far from enough. You needed to have him totally, every ounce of him—his body, mind, and soul to help quiet your inner turmoil. Not a fragment of him could you share with anyone. You could not even let him have that part of himself that he needed to be a human being. You failed to understand that no man—no human being—can be totally given away, not even in marriage.

He left you because he needed room to breathe and room to grow. He would have shriveled up or suffocated if he had stayed. You knew this, because you told him to leave over and over again so that he might live.

Becky, I find it very hard to say good-bye to you. I cringe to think of your last night alone. How horribly lonely you must have been! This is beyond me to bear.

When I referred you to a psychiatrist, and when at midnight I had you hospitalized, I knew this hurt you just terribly. Becky, I did that because I cared, but you couldn't understand. You felt only the rejection of being labeled "mentally ill," and that was far more than you could take.

I remember the many beautiful sessions we had together also. For a number of months you came so gladly and cheerfully. We were so hopeful that the loneliness that had been hounding you since childhood would at last leave you. You were making plans to go to architectural school. Then you lost your apartment and finally your job. Getting fired was the last thing you needed at this stage in life. Soon you started crumbling again.

Becky, we didn't want you to leave. We needed you. You were one of us. You were our child, our wife, our sister, our friend. Your leaving diminishes us because you were a part of us. We are less because you are gone.

The way you left makes your leaving even harder. It makes saying good-bye so difficult. It's so confusing. We want to blame ourselves, or each other, or *you, but we cannot. We are hurting enough without hurting each other more. And I know you wouldn't want us to hurt more, for you knew hurt too well.*

So good-bye, Becky. We hope to meet you again. Forgive us wherein we failed you. We forgive you for your error. Good-bye, Becky!"

During the reading there was a gradual increase in the amount of crying. Every few moments someone sobbed audibly. Her father broke into a loud sob when I bid my final good-bye. My own voice broke several times. I let my tears roll without interference. I simply kept reading slowly.

As I think about it now, my message was a simple one. To those who were gathered in Becky's memory, I had given a message of comfort in their hour of need. "God is with you now. In the midst of your heartache and sorrow, God is with you now."

As I began leaving the lectern, the pastor quickly rose to his feet and took over. Confident now, he needed no notes. His voice was clear and distinct. He was looking heavenward as if he were talking to God as he said, "Let us pray!"

Oh, God, we come to you at this moment when we need you most. We pray for all of us, for we have erred. We failed to extend a hand to Becky when she needed us. When she still was in our midst we hardly knew her. Forgive us, Father! We also pray for churches and their people, for we hardly know how many more like Becky may be among us. People are dying because we don't care. We don't even know them. Move us to care, Father, so that Becky's death will not have been in vain, but that we may wake from our lethargy.

God, we pray that you will receive Becky and

*grant her the peace that she hardly knew on earth—
and I commit her soul into your care because we
know you care far more than we do. Amen.*

After every death it is essential to permit God to
enter the healing process. At times this means making
explicit choices, like reaching out to other people who
have experienced similar losses. Then, one's grief becomes the means for helping others grieve more effectively. Also, misfortunes may be translated into build-
ing blocks for the kingdom of God.

There are times when all we can do is open ourselves and watch as God steps into the tragedy and
performs a miracle. All we need to do is believe what we
experience.

Mending a broken heart after suicide is one of the
most difficult processes to go through. It may be
extremely difficult to see God at work. People feel so
buffeted by the experience. If ever there is helplessness, it is after such a death. However, it also provides
the greatest opportunity to turn the future over to
God.

Suicide is baffling, especially when the person is a
relative or a close friend. For the survivor, suicide
leaves so many questions unanswered. The person one
needs to ask is gone. So friends and family are left
alone, second-guessing the answers. Why did she do
it? What did I do wrong? What if I had said or done
something different? Would she be living now? Then,
finally, when all else fails: God, why did you let her do
it? We may torture ourselves; yet there are no answers.
Finally, we may despair.

God, in his own mysterious way, often steps into all
this confusion and acts, transforming lives. Then all
we can do is yield to God in love. We also learn that we

must respond with total compassion at all times. The deeper the pain, the greater is the need for love. The tragedy of suicide is the last place where edicts of condemnation are needed. Rather, love must flow so the healing of God may occur.

In my earlier book *Dialogue with Death* (no longer in print) the chapter "Dialogue with Suicide" drew the largest response as well as the most affirmation and controversy. The most frequent reaction from Christians was negative. They challenged this statement in the eulogy of Becky: "I have confidence that God grants some people the right not to live."

Theologically, this notion is questionable and so it became the subject of debate. Although I made this statement, I do not have a final answer. God alone is omniscient and the final Judge. What I do know is that after I had walked through some of the last horrible miles with Becky and felt compelled to speak at her funeral, I felt led by God to say this. The few relatives and friends were devastated enough. I could not inflict further harm upon them. I felt led to represent a loving, compassionate God.

Recently, after reading my eulogy, a pastor wrote this letter to me: "It is very difficult for me to say that a person would be lost to the kingdom because of an act of suicide. After having been involved in a psychiatric clinic where at least 50 to 100 patients who attempted suicide were treated, I cannot outright close the door on such a person, and I don't think God would either.

"The desperation that drives a person to that phase is beyond description and no loving God would judge an individual on the basis of the final act alone.

"God is not unmindful of the circumstances surrounding anyone's life or death."

People have repeatedly told us of pastors, relatives,

and friends who remembered this chapter when they were forced to deal with suicide. Then they reread it, quoted it, and even read the eulogy at the funeral. At that moment every sentence seemed perfectly understandable and felt like a gift from God to them.

In our travels, many times someone makes the connection between the well-known eulogy and the author. With gratitude another account of its use to bring comfort is described and we yield to greater forces. I bow my head in thanksgiving and say, "God is still at work in this world."

After the events of Becky's death were over, it was hard to see that God had been at work in these events. I knew that I felt led to deliver the eulogy. It seemed the only way to care for these few friends and relatives in the cold atmosphere of the funeral home. I had to tell them that the God I know does not turn away at the time of such intense suffering. God is there even in the greatest tragedy.

The mending of God came as an aftermath. The divine healing drama was unfolding far away—in Texas where another Becky had committed suicide.

I became aware of these events when I received the following letter:

Dear Dr. Schmitt,

I want to share the role your book Dialogue with Death, *has served recently.*

A student gave me the book to read after Sunday school class a few weeks ago. Her name was Becky. Reluctantly (because of a busy schedule), I read the book and gained a lot. Last week another friend's daughter committed suicide. Her name was Becky.

While trying to compose a note to the grieving mother, I recalled your chapter on suicide and your eulogy to Becky. I gave it to the mother to read.

Yesterday my pastor and two other friends told me that had helped the mother's suffering and given her a more comfortable memory than anything anyone else has said or done. She rereads it daily. Isn't it wonderful how God uses people to help others? I'm a Becky, too.

It is beyond my human comprehension how this could have happened. I can only say that I believe God was present.

Randomly, I had selected the name Becky to disguise the identity of the actual person. A second Becky had read the account and felt compelled to take it to her Sunday school teacher, another Becky, and insist that she read it. Then the suicide of a young woman, also a Becky, became part of this chain of events.

This Becky's mother, in her intense grief over the loss of her daughter, saw God at work mending her brokenness. She too wrote to me:

Dr. Schmitt,
  Your book, and the circumstances that caused it to be placed in our hands have done more to lift us and give us strength than anything that has happened during our loss of our Becky. Thank God, thank God. He has used you in such a wonderful and special way....

One touching event needs to be shared from her lengthy letter. At the graveside service, the mother longed for a sign to feel God's presence with certainty. With keen spiritual discernment, she heard the voice of God in what might have gone unnoticed.

I want to tell you about her [Becky's] funeral service, which was a graveside service. There was a cedar tree right next to the canopy which was only about eight feet high. During the time when the pastor was talking and people were all around that little tree, a songbird came down and sat on that tree and sang his little heart out. I believe that it was a message sent from God to comfort us. It was so unusual, so unlike what a bird would do with humans around. That incident gives me a great hope that our Becky is now where she will never be unhappy again.

I believe that we must let God do the mending, but that he uses people to carry out his healing.

It was important for me to go to the first Becky's funeral. Through the eulogy I took the relatives and friends on a journey back. I had to retell the story of Becky as I had understood it. In doing that, I was able to get past the horrible events of the nature of the death, and renew their acquaintance with the Becky we all had known before the suicide.

I became part of the post-death ritual. We were at a critical moment. Immediately behind us was the awful memory, and before us was the bleak future. I sought God's help as I stepped into this critical situation—to help these people bring closure to the past and step into the future with greater peace. At times like these we need to obey courageously what we sense God is calling us to do.

As for the events in Texas, I simply marvel at the unique circumstances. I attribute them to the supernatural working of God in this world. I want to believe that there are times when God steps into history and changes events, so that we will not forget that God is still at work. I sensed the spiritual meaning of these events, and that gave me the courage to reaffirm that

God was directing the Sunday School teacher and reassuring this Becky's mother in her grief.

In all correspondence with this mother, I aided her to take God's hand and embark on an emotional journey returning to reflect on the tragedy. The most recent journey occurred in relation to this chapter, eight years after the tragic experience.

To find God in suffering we must open our spiritual eyes, look beyond the natural events, and refuse to believe that everything is coincidental—just as Becky's grieving mother heard the bird sing at the graveside service, and in her heart translated it into a benediction from God upon this event. As she pondered this in her heart over the years, she permitted God to do the mending. She was enabled to let go of her only daughter—her beloved Becky.

As this mother listened for God in the song of a bird, she has listened for God in her life, and in the lives of other people. Not only has God been mending her heart, she and her husband have relocated to enter full time Christian service and are devoting their lives to bring healing to others.

A Lengthy Process

How long does it take to mend a broken heart? It depends on many factors. It took Sara 16 years. Her desperate need for the lost loved one made letting go extremely difficult.

At 13, Sara was a lonely child until she discovered true brotherly love in Ivan, her sibling who was one year younger. In him she found her first true and trusted confidant. Then, a year later, he died. This was a perfect setup for an enormously difficult separation process.

As was customary in her rural conservative Amish-Mennonite community, emotions were endured but not talked about. As a result, Sara had quite a poor sense of personhood. Her self-worth was largely built on the mutual respect of her brother. Then, when he was gone, nothing was left. She was an empty shell.

Sara chose to build a wall around herself and vowed that no one would ever get inside. She determined never again to become vulnerable. She had risked it once, and that ended in tragedy and ceaseless pain; so she would never do it again.

After the tragedy, Sara completed high school in her home community. Next, she did a highly unusual thing for persons in her church. She chose to go to college. She could easily perform the outward motions to the highest expectations of the teachers. Her inner self was hidden behind her conservative dress. This difference in garb kept her peer group at a distance, since they found it difficult to understand her.

No one knew the person in the shell. No one knew how lonely she was. They would not ask, because her demeanor told them not to. The death of her brother had completely paralyzed her. Since she knew of no way to be rescued, she chose to remain there. She also resolved that no one would ever know about her emotional paralysis.

I met her seven years after her brother had died. At that point no one had asked her to tell all about her loss, so I did. It took nine more years for her to recover from her futile suffering. If someone had intervened sooner, the healing could have been more rapid.

To let go of her brother who had died, Sara would have to tell the story over and over until she was free. I helped her chart her experience and explained why she had to relive every event of the tragedy, even every emotion she had ever felt (see chapter 9).

For three years we walked through her grief journey by letters, returning to the death scene and her pattern of survival over and over again. Here are parts of her letters to me:

January 15, 1974
I deeply appreciated the opportunity to chat with you. It meant a lot to me. I want you to know that your caring means so much to me. Especially, I appreciate that you took time to really care about my hurts and were willing to listen to my hurts and losses.

It does make a lot of sense, but I've discovered it to be a rather painful experience to relive the events in my memory again. I am willing to do it if this brings healing, even if it's difficult. It isn't as difficult when one can share it with a trusted and confidential friend. Thanks so much for being that friend to me.

Ivan and I shared numerous joyful times together,

and I am thankful for each one of them. We just became very close about a year before his death. We did a lot of talking together, and we enjoyed doing things together. We enjoyed going away together. What one liked, the other did also.

The thing I missed the most after his passing was that I could no longer talk with him about joys as well as hurts and problems. No one else quite understood like Ivan, and I still keep telling myself just that. Whenever we felt hurt in any way, we could confide in each other without anyone else knowing. We trusted each other completely. Ivan's two great mentors were Abraham Lincoln and Thomas Edison. He dreamed of becoming an inventor someday. He loved to do scientific experiments. We spent lots of time talking about hopes, dreams, desires.

I really can't put into words what a great loss it was for me to lose Ivan. Because it was so deep, I don't know quite how to explain it.

The last evening we spent together was at my aunt's place. Then he went camping with several of his chums. They wanted to go camping before school started. They were riding bicycles in the dark, and he went down over a wooden bridge—about a six-foot drop. He went across some rocks and hit his head against an old hickory post—so hard that the imprints of his glasses were left on the post. He walked about a half a mile to a residence of one of the boys, and they took him to the hospital to have him checked.

The only thing you could see was a cut above his left eye. This was Thursday evening, September 1, 1966. They called my parents. Since it was supposedly nothing serious, only Dad went out to the hospital. Ivan was resting well, so Dad came home about 4:00 a.m. because they thought it wasn't necessary for him to stay.

The next morning they were going to X-ray for a possible skull fracture; but then he began vomiting, and it was too late. He became unconscious, so they made quick plans to transfer him to a larger hospital.

My two brothers and I didn't find out about his mishap until morning— which would have been Friday morning. Perhaps that was for the good. No one will ever know how it hurt to find that out and see his clothes all cut up when I got up in the morning. Maybe I should say that was hurt number one in the whole deal.

They transferred him to a larger hospital in the ambulance. A brain specialist checked him and thought about possible surgery, but Friday afternoon about three o'clock, he quit breathing on his own; so they put him on a respirator.

After this happened, Dad called us kids at home and told us about the seriousness of Ivan's condition. Mom and Dad were at the hospital, and we were home by ourselves. Surgery was of course canceled after he quit breathing on his own.

That cut like a knife when Dad called us. One of my brothers answered the phone, and Dad said we should come to the hospital immediately. He also said that the doctor said that Ivan probably would not live. That was almost more than we could bear, because for the first time we faced the possibility of his death.

So we quickly got ready and went that 35 mile stretch to the hospital. That was the saddest trip we kids had ever taken by ourselves. It hurt badly!

Early Monday morning Dad called and told Mom to come to the hospital because Ivan was in his final moments. So someone from church took Mom, and my oldest brother and I stayed home to take care of some much needed duties. Then, about 9:30 a.m. on Monday, Ivan died.

May 30, 1974

I believe one hurt I experienced was that we kids had little if any say about the funeral plans. My parents and our pastor decided all that. I think one reason it hurt me was that I loved Ivan very very deeply and there were certain things I would have liked to have done in remembrance of him. The communication was on a doing level rather than a feeling level in our family.

Suddenly the pressure blew the lid off my can of emotions, and my pent-up feelings exploded. So I cried and cried after I knew I was alone and no one would be aware of my pain. You know, Abe, as I look back—way back there—I was establishing a pattern of hiding my true feelings at a young age.

Some of the girls volunteered to stay with me overnight, but I refused everyone of them because that was the only time I really cried and let my real feelings out.

It was a hard night for me because I dreaded the funeral very very much! I never shared my grief with anyone. I felt God was punishing me by taking my brother, because I knew I wasn't all that God wanted me to be.

The hardest moment for me was when I saw Ivan for the last time—that about tore me up. I cried a little, more than anyone had seen me cry in public through the whole process. But I quickly brushed it aside because I thought it wasn't acceptable to show my real emotions through tears. I am praying that God will help me to release some of my hurts through crying because I see it as healthy healing therapy.

Abe, in all my life I never hurt so much as that moment. I felt like the bottom fell out of my world as I left the cemetery. I never felt so alone in all my life. We came back home and shared a meal with our friends and relatives. There were lots of people, but eating sure wasn't my bag right then. I ate basically to be polite to our friends. Eventually everybody left in the evening, and there we were all alone. It seemed so empty that you could have almost heard the walls crack. In a way it was a relief that it was over with at last. If I was ever tired, it was then. That whole experience just sapped my energy. I was just about done for. We all went to bed early.

Gradually life came back to normal, and I just had to act like nothing really happened. If only I would have had a friend who would have understood my feelings and helped me work through my grief.

The pain is intensified when in the initial state of shock fellow Christians quote Scripture and give biblical reasons why tragedies happen. One of the best examples is, "It was God's will." This only intensified my anger toward God and the people around me. God is in control at all times. However, he allows certain things to happen that aren't in his will. Tragedies and hurts in this life are the inevitable result of a fallen world and fallen human beings.

What I needed most at that time was not a lot of advice, but people who would listen and be present with their warmth and silence. In addition, the power of touch works miracles in our lives at such a time. Although we as Christians have God and the Word and prayer and the Holy Spirit to help us in these times of need, we need love with flesh on it. I believe love in the flesh puts an arm around bereaved persons and weeps with them.

Writing this letter was extremely difficult. I suppose that's why I kept putting it off, but God kept prompting me that I must do it. So today I decided to write.

I would enjoy writing you another twenty pages on what God's been doing in my life in the last four months. God's been doing some interesting things in my life lately. I can say from the depth of my heart I've never experienced a greater peace and joy.

April 15, 1975

*When you last saw me I was a rather shy, re-
served, naive somebody. But I'm glad to tell you I feel
like a new person since I met you. I was able to work
through much of my inner frustrations and tensions
at college, and life for me today is an exciting adventure. I've found a new freedom in Jesus Christ. How
I'd love to sit down and share with you some of the
goodness of God in my life, especially in the last year
and a half. God certainly is good to me!*

In the eleventh year, I was scheduled to conduct a
workshop to train people in the art of listening. Much
to my shock, Sara showed up. For the first day she
clearly held a distance. She had brought a group of
friends with her and she remained close to them. She
needed them to protect herself from me.

When I found her alone at an unguarded moment,
she suddenly poured out her struggle again in spite of
her fear. Then, I asked her to share her story with the
entire group. I assured her that I would guide her
through the whole venture and would ask specific
questions; at no time would she be left speechless or
stranded. I also said I would sit with her and she could
face me as if we were having a personal interview. I
assured her that I had done this often and it had
proved to be a powerful teaching tool to demonstrate
the listening skills that I meant to teach the group.
She consented because I needed her.

That Saturday evening proved to be a profound
experience for everyone. It demonstrated the power of
listening to transform lives. We could talk about the
exact nature of the death, Sara's years of silent
paralysis, and how one encounter with a listener had
enabled changes to occur during the next three years.

For the remainder of the workshop, we dealt with other subjects. However, Sara had won the hearts of the entire group. As people talked in the formal sessions, they often returned to the events of Saturday night to make their points.

During the informal periods Sara no longer needed her friends to protect her. People kept clustering around her to get more and more from her. They wanted to demonstrate Christian compassion, but they also wanted to learn the secret she had guarded all these years. If they could understand her, then perhaps they could understand themselves better.

Sara's growth continued.

May 11, 1977
I've done a lot of thinking since the weekend, and sometimes it almost "blows my mind" to think about all that happened there. All that affirmation and caring did something for me, and I praise God for it. I felt nothing but love and acceptance from that group. It was such an encouragement to me because in my home community affirmation was limited. I felt like a whole person with a new lease on life. I felt like the Scripture in Deuteronomy 30:19, where death and life were set before the people. I now felt free to choose life and get on with living again.

It's strange how sometimes our greatest hurts turn out to be our most precious gifts to share with others!

My whole idea of death has certainly changed. Before, I couldn't think of anything more horrid than death and funerals. Now, believe it or not, I've actually gone to some funerals and felt very comfortable.

Now I can honestly say being a Christian is the greatest thing that's ever happened to me and I enjoy life in the midst of problems. I love people and I love

*to reach out and minister to other people who are in
need. This hasn't happened overnight, but it's been a
gradual journey.*

*Thanks for having confidence in me to ask me to
share with the group. You'll never know what that
meant. After we got started, I felt as relaxed as could
be. Words fail to express my deepest gratitude and
thanks to you. . . .*

*A deeper healing took place when I shared my
story in a group setting because of the intense compassionate caring that flowed from this group to me.*

*I just thought tonight that if it weren't for you, I
probably wouldn't be a Christian. Furthermore, I
probably would have ended it all long ago, or I'd be
in some mental hospital. Thanks so much for making
me feel like perhaps there was yet something worth-
while to live for. When I was literally down and out,
feeling life wasn't worth living, you gave me hope!*

Fourteen years after the loss of her brother, Sara
was ready to tackle her problem with obesity. The success of this meant that she was also ready to change
her style of clothing and lifestyle.

February 14, 1980
*I began working with my weight problem by at-
tending Weight Watchers once a week. I've lost almost 40 pounds now, and I've got about 30 more to
take off until I reach my goal. I cannot begin to tell
you how much better I feel about myself. My family's
never-ending support kept me from quitting when the
temptation became great. Mother has been a real inspiration to me through the whole process, thus im-
~~ing our relationship.*

*, ~e found out a lot about myself in this process. I
~cluded that I was living to eat rather than eating
~ ~ve. For me, eating was merely a crutch to com-
pensate for my inner struggles. For years I blamed*

other people for the problem, but I finally came to the painful conclusion that I had to take ownership of my problem. Sometimes I wonder why we as Christians are so hard on the alcoholic and the smoker, but somehow we don't see obesity as being equally harmful to our bodies.

The other week I told Mom that I wish I knew what it's like to be thin. She said she remembered a time before Ivan's death when I was thin. In fact she has a picture of me that was taken the week before Ivan's death that proves it. That was real interesting to me. After she told me, I concluded that this is just another step in the healing process of working through his death, without me having been aware of it.

The final letter from Sara arrived in the sixteenth year. Her own words show that her grief is completed and her broken heart is mended. She is a person in her own right, who can live effectively without Ivan.

December 16, 1982

I am experiencing a peace with life that I never knew existed, with the feeling that there's no hidden agenda and no feeling like I want to get away from it all as I used to have. I just want to be open to God to whatever he has for me. God's presence is so much more real since that anger and resentment are gone. It feels so good just to be me!

It feels good to experience a sense of wholeness. Our mission is to be God's person and know we're truly loved by God. The longer I live, the more important I believe it is to be rather than to do. I want to seek to be God's person in the coming years.

May the God of grace be with you.

May the lordship of Christ possess you.

And may the Spirit of promise sustain you.

> *Lovingly,*
> *Sara*

The same culture that created the dilemma for Sara also taught her to be stalwart and strong—to persevere and never surrender. When Sara had found these attributes could be used to deal with grief, she was able to move through the grief process. An additional benefit was that she won a lot of friends.

Sometimes people need to deal with the loss as dramatically as they experienced the intensity of the loss. For Sara, this happened as she and her story of grief became the central drama at a workshop.

How often must a person replay the story of a lost loved one? How long does it take? Will it ever be forgotten?

Sara needed to relive the story of her loss many times. It took more than a decade for her to let go of Ivan, but she may never be able to forget him.

When someone is emotionally dependent on another person, the pain is very intense at the time of death. In addition, Sara's brother died during her mid-teens—a time when dependency on peers is essential for growth. The violence and suddenness with which Ivan died added further complications. This was intensified by a culture which did little to recognize the emotional dimension of people at the time of loss.

When we make ourselves available to be used as God's instruments in healing grief, we diminish the length of time persons are disabled by the grieving process.

Turn Again to Life

Life is often described as a road upon which we must travel. We can choose to go in only one direction, and we can never return. Time prohibits us from reliving any segment of life. We may return only through memories, but that too is at the expense of moving further ahead on the road of life.

This truth hits us most harshly at the moment of a death. In one split second all of life is different. There is no resemblance to the past, and the future is unknown and new. Even though we might wish to repeat a relationship lost by death, we cannot. There are only awesome choices. How can life go on? How can we not give in to despair? How can we choose to take the path of hope and optimism with a renewed reason for living? How can we turn again to life?

As we travel on this road of life, we meet many others who walk with us. Sometimes the journey is brief. Someone may walk alongside for a specific reason and then our paths part. Most of the time this is perfectly acceptable. Each must go his or her own way.

There are times when we find walking together more meaningful and we travel together longer. Our parents were crucial to the earliest portion of this journey. As time passes, parents and children gradually go on different roads. We still watch each other's path, and we continue to be affected by each other's walk. If all goes well, our parents travel on the road for a long time. When this is true, we find it easier when they leave. Life may become more burdensome than the struggle seems worth. We grieve the loss but it is easy to go on, perhaps with only fleeting memories.

Then there are meetings on the road of life that are not as casual. The most significant ones involve a mate or a child. Here the nature of the walk is drastically affected by the other person or persons. Often the other's need to take a certain path may determine the path we take.

As we affect and permit ourselves to be affected by these people, a more meaningful relationship develops. Our characters are shaped by these traveling companions. As time passes, these paths become so intertwined that it becomes impossible to determine whose path is being followed.

In the course of natural events our children begin taking paths that lead them away from us. We remain confident that their choices for the remainder of the journey will be deeply affected by what happened when they walked with us. Under these conditions their leaving is usually easy to accept.

With a mate the paths of life may be so close that for periods of time we forget that there are two. We assume that this journey will last for a long time. We say these paths will continue together "until death do us part."

The truth is that death does part people on the road of life, regardless of how casual or how intense the relationships may have been. There is a problem when death occurs at an inappropriate stage in life—when we are least prepared to part. When we still need the other person to find our way, there is a major crisis.

After the death of someone close to us, we come to a fork in the road. At that crossroad, we must make a significant choice. We can go either to the left or to the right. Often neither of these is what we really desire.

If we had our preference, we would want to have the parent, friend, mate, or child back with us again. However, that is impossible. Death is final, and the road for the departed one has ended.

Another choice has to be made. How will the future be lived without one's loved one? In most cases the choice is either to turn away from life or to turn again to life.

If a loved one was turned away from life by death, then why should the survivor not turn away from life also? This road is marked by pain, depression, despair, and even wanting to die. To take this road briefly is a natural response to a loss. But turning away from life cannot be a permanent choice. At some point one must take the other fork marked by hope, optimism, and a renewal.

The central message of this book is that people can choose the unnatural direction after any death—no matter how tragic—and turn again to life.

The difficulty in turning again to life is that it is not a matter of coming to a crossroad and selecting the "road of life" or the "road of despair." It is better to turn around and return in memory. It is helpful to go back to the beginning of the lost relationship and to slowly relive every milestone along the way as you return. The key is to experience both painful and joyful memories.

At times the road will get rough as you approach the stretch marked "pre-death process." This may have occurred when you discovered that your loved one was ill, or perhaps terminally ill. The signs were pointing toward death. Now each moment became precious and every sentence was engraved in stone. Then the moment of death arrived.

For some this stretch of road was missed because there was no warning. Life with a loved one ceased in one split second. After one slip on the stairway, life with Drew ended for Joyce (chapter 6). In these situations the next milestone is even more difficult to pass. This portion is marked "death."

At this point in the journey it is helpful to stop and reflect for a while. Here the road which preceded and the road which will follow have little resemblance. From that moment on life has to be lived without the loved one.

It is almost incomprehensible to reflect on what a death really means—that one person while living can have so great an impact. Each change of mood has an effect. Each word spoken can hurt or heal. The complexity of a human relationship is infinitely variable. It can bring us to the pinnacle of joy and may feel like a foretaste of heaven. It also may result in utter despair and may cause us to wonder whether life is worth living.

Then, after the final breath that person is gone—totally gone. The whole drama surrounding the person—the unique personality as well as the entire relationship is gone. The only part of the departed one that remains is in our memories, and even that fades rapidly. This should motivate us to pause and reflect for a long time.

After this, grieving persons move on to a somewhat smoother portion of road. In the "post-death ritual" stretch of the journey we meet others who need to let go. These persons remain close to us. They are careful and thoughtful because they know we are hurting. It is good to pause and look at the guest book to see who signed it, and ponder what went through their minds as they said good-bye to the one close to us.

Then it is on to "the business as usual" portion of the road. This would not be so bad if you could live as before. However, it means going on alone, and that is tough. It also means being reminded over and over again that you are without the loved one. At the most unexpected and inappropriate times there are flashbacks, with all the emotions in tow. There is the need to burst into tears at the wrong time and place. Just when you thought you had climbed over the mountain, you go around another turn in the road and the raw emotions caused by the loss emerge again. It is not that you have not made progress; it is only that the nature of grief trips you so often.

It is helpful to think of this part of the road as winding around a mountain. You should expect the same scenes to come into view, but as you look down you will see that the road spirals and you are at a higher level than before. The feelings are the same, but you can reflect on them more objectively from another vantage point.

Finally you come to the present and discover that you have made progress on the road of life. You have chosen to live again.

However, the journey does not end here. You must go back over and over again. Many, many trips must be taken until you have made peace with the past and you are ready to live again with hope.

It is necessary to go back, in memory, over and over again. At times the journey begins when you find yourself walking to the window at the the time when the loved one usually returned home. You expect your partner or child to come home again, but that is not possible. Then a journey back is necessary, with special emphasis on what it really meant for you to have him or her arrive. It is even appropriate to visualize what it would mean at that exact moment if a return visit were possible. Then allow yourself to experience the feelings of the loss in their true intensity.

Essentially, grief work is reliving a past relationship until you can let go and reach out to the future for new relationships.

After all I have shared in this book, what can I add? Only a reminder that the power to turn again to life is conveyed in the Book of Life.

POSTLUDE

What, then, shall we say
   in response to death?
If God is for us,
   who can be against us?
Who shall separate us
   from the love of Christ?
Shall trouble or hardship
   or heartache, or sorrow
   or loneliness or despair or pain?
No, in all these things
   we are more than conquerors
   through him who loved us.
For I am convinced
   that neither death nor life,
Neither sickness nor accident,
   neither the present nor the future
   nor any adversity,
Neither grief nor loss,
   nor anything else in all creation
Will be able to separate us
   from the love of God
That is in Christ Jesus our Lord.
  —Adapted from Romans 8:31-39, NIV

OTHER HERALD PRESS RESOURCES ON DEATH

Danger in the Pines by Ruth Nulton Moore. Juvenile novel of 14-year-old Jeff Dawson coming to terms with his mother's new friend after his father's tragic death. 160 pages.

Empty Arms by Mary Joyce Rae. Visitation Pamphlet for those who lose their child at birth or through miscarriage. 16 pages.

Gina In-Between by Dorothy Hamilton. Juvenile novel about a father's death and the idea that the mother may remarry.

Grief's Slow Work by Harold Bauman. Visitation Pamphlet explaining the process one normally goes through following bereavement. 16 pages.

Helping Children Cope with Death, by Robert V. Dodd. 56 pages.

In Grief's Lone Hour by John M. Drescher. Visitation Pamphlet providing understanding of the grief experience. 16 pages.

Morning Joy by Helen Good Brenneman. Meditations for those who have suffered loss—whether it be through death, divorce, ill health, or economic disaster. 80 pages.

My Walk Through Grief by Janette Klopfenstein. The story of a young mother's sudden loss of her husband. 120 pages.

Remember the Eagle Day by Guenn Martin. Junior high adventure involving the death of Grandpa Jake, God's loving care, and moving on with life.

Tell Me About Death, Mommy, by Janette Klopfenstein. A young widow's story of helping her sons cope with their father's death. 112 pages.

THE AUTHOR

Dr. Abraham Schmitt is uniquely qualified to give leadership in the field of death and grief. Academically he holds advance degrees in social work from the University of Pennsylvania and in theology from Goshen Biblical Seminary. In his personal life he has not been forced to deal with dying or grieving, so he has chosen to pursue it as a specialty. Because his interest in this field is widely known, his clinical practice includes many clients struggling with loss.

Currently he is involved in three areas of service. His private practice includes individual and marriage therapy with preference given to issues of death and grief. Workshops conducted in United States and Canada include subjects of death and dying, grief and loss, marriage and family issues, and congregational caring. The third facet is writing for publication. His most recent books, written jointly with his wife, Dorothy, are *When a Congregation Cares: A New Approach to Crisis Ministry* and *Renewing Family Life: In Search of a Silver Lining.*

Abe grew up in an Old Colony Mennonite village in Saskatchewan, Canada. In this setting, death and grief could not be disguised. The intense kinship system forced everyone, including children, to participate in everyone's victories as well as their tragedies.

After leaving the Mennonite reserve he attended Rosthern Junior College, Canadian Mennonite College, and Saskatchewan Normal School. In the United States he graduated from Goshen College and

Goshen College Biblical Seminary. He received his master's and doctor's degrees from the University of Pennsylvania.

This final degree led to a professorship in the Department of Psychiatry, the School of Social Work, and the Marriage Council, where he created their first interdisciplinary course on death and dying.